Erie
Lackawanna
In Color

Volume 7:
Mahoning Division

Stephen M. Timko

Published by
Morning Sun Books, Inc.
9 Pheasant Lane
Scotch Plains, NJ 07076
Printed in Korea

Library of Congress
Catalog Card No. 91-060917

First Printing
ISBN 1-58248-348-5

To access our full library *In Color* visit us at
www.morningsunbooks.com

ROBERT J. YANOSEY, President

DEDICATION

This book is dedicated to the employees of the Erie Lackawanna's Mahoning Division. Those covered by this dedication were and still are my friends, coworkers and unknown associates. As a new employee in 1965 I knew few of my peers but made new acquaintances daily. Those contacts fostered my learning through their teachings or by my own observations of them performing their daily duties. Their friendship and assistance resulted in my successful advancement, resulting in a 43-year railroad career. It was through their able guidance that I learned the Mahoning Division inside and out. Thank-you, my fellow coworkers!

ACKNOWLEDGEMENTS

I wish to thank the Erie Lackawanna Historical Society's Archives Committee for making this assortment of slides possible. Their dedication to the history of the Erie Lackawanna has permitted me to fulfill a longtime dream to provide a photographic slideshow of the Mahoning Division. Of course, the ELHS would not have been able to provide these photos if it were not for the photographers that recorded the scenes. So, thanks also go to David Shaw, Mike Kopach, William Herrmann, Ron Rohrbaugh, David Hamley, and the many others who saw fit to donate their collections to the society. I'd also like to acknowledge several long-time friends and coworkers who assisted with details: Cal Banse for his firsthand knowledge of the division, Michael Connor for his history of the Mahoning Division and assistance with several captions, retired locomotive engineer Loyd Mitchell and retired conductor Jerry Heckman for assisting with details and employee names, and Steve Twarogowski of the ELHS for providing traffic and commodity figures and details. And last but not least, thank-you, Bob Yanosey of Morning Sun Books for publishing this project.

PAGE 1 • Nothing says Mahoning Division better than an Alco and a Dunmore caboose. The locomotive, an Alco model Century 424, was new to the EL in the spring of 1963. Delivered in EL's freight scheme of black and yellow, all 15 eventually obtained the later more colorful scheme. All of the class MFA-24-D-6 survived to see Conrail in 1976 but were quickly retired to streamline the new railroad's roster. The welded caboose was built by the Erie's Dunmore, PA car shops immediately after World War II. They served the Erie, EL and Conrail well, many of them for up to 50 years. The equipment in this photo is assigned to a North Randall Hump Crew and is seen in the Pocket Track across from the North Randall Depot in the summer of 1976. *(Ron Rohrbaugh, ELHS Archives Collection)*

ABOUT THE AUTHOR

I lived within view of both the First and Second Sub-Division in Warren during my younger years. Growing up, I was a frequent visitor to the Warren Passenger Station as well as Leavittsburg Yard and SN Jct. Upon graduation from high school in 1965, I applied for and received a position as Extra Operator—Mahoning Division, working at all of the interlocking towers and at several agencies between Meadville and Kent and Cleveland. In 1967 extra train dispatchers were required so I swiftly qualified between Salamanca and Hornell, NY, and shortly thereafter on the balance of the division. The Chief Dispatcher's chair was next.

With the combining of former EL and PC offices in Youngstown in 1979, Conrail's new Youngstown Division was formed. I was promoted to the position of Supervisor of Operating Rules in 1984 and in 1988 I was transferred to the same position in Pittsburgh. In 1989 a promotion to Lead Trainmaster in Youngstown gave me responsibility for the entire former Mahoning Division between Kent, OH and Corry, PA, as well as other former PC territory. In 1996 the General Manager tapped me to work in the Division Office in Pittsburgh as Manager of Operations Planning and in 2000 Norfolk Southern promoted me to Assistant Superintendent –Train Operations in Pittsburgh.

After accepting a buyout, I formed Beaver Valley Rail, a railroad consulting company. I was invited to join the newly formed Western New York & Pennsylvania RR, which was reopening the former EL line between Meadville and Hornell. Later, I became Vice President & General Manager of that line with headquarters at Falconer, NY where I oversaw the daily operations and rebirth of the new road from a 10-MPH route with 50 serviceable miles to a 40-MPH line with nearly 250 miles of trackage.

After retirement from railroad service in 2006, I still consult for industries and shortline railroads. *Erie Lackawanna's Mahoning Division In Color* is my thirteenth Morning Sun Books publication.

RECOMMENDED READING

- *Trackside around Cleveland with Dave McKay*, by Dave McKay
- *Trackside around Youngstown with Dave McKay* by Stephen M. Timko
- *Trackside in the Rust Belt with Cal Banse* by Stephen M. Timko
- *Trackside in Eastern Ohio with Dave McKay* by Stephen M. Timko
- *Erie Railroad Facilities, Volume 3: Pennsylvania-Ohio-Indiana* by Robert J. Yanosey
- *Erie Railroad in Color, Volume 2* by Stephen M. Timko

Erie Lackawanna *In Color*

Volume 7: Mahoning Division

FOREWORD
By Michael J. Connor

For most of its life the Erie Lackawanna Railroad's 2,916.71-mile system[1] was composed of six[2] operating divisions. Of these, the 708.6 miles of the Mahoning Division were almost inarguably the most interesting and diverse on the EL. Those miles certainly were the most important—the Erie Railroad, whose merger with the Delaware, Lackawanna & Western on October 17, 1960 formed the Erie Lackawanna, proudly proclaimed that it served the "Heart of Industrial America." And nowhere on the Erie/EL did that industrial heart beat stronger and more openly than on the Mahoning Division.

Mahoning Division crews served the steel mills of the Mahoning River valley, the oil refineries of northwest Pennsylvania, bituminous coal mines in northern Pennsylvania and northeast Ohio, and myriads of other manufacturing and agricultural customers in 153[3] Mahoning Division communities. But on-line customers were just a part of the Mahoning Division's work—the Erie/EL's fleet of passenger trains between Hoboken (Jersey City) and Chicago, again, almost inarguably the best trains in the Northeast, and Pittsburgh-to-Cleveland (and Detroit), and fast through-freight trains between Chicago and New York/New England all moved swiftly and safely across the Mahoning's rails.

The Mahoning Division's history was the story of the 55 railroads that built and operated portions of its track. The incorporation of the New York & Erie Rail-Road Company (NY&E) on April 24, 1832 started the Mahoning Division story. The construction of the NY&E was a long and challenging progress but success finally came on April 9, 1851, when the last spike was driven at Cuba Summit, N.Y. (Mile Post JC 377.5), opening the NY&E's original Piermont-to-Dunkirk, N.Y. Main Line. Setting the tone for much of what became the Mahoning Division, the NY&E was built to a 6-foot gauge—it would be almost thirty years before the railroad would be standard gauged.

One of the more obscure portions of the Erie Lackawanna was the line from Carrollton, N.Y. south (railroad east) to Bradford and the coal fields of northwestern Pennsylvania. The incorporation of The Buffalo & Bradford Railroad Company (B&B) on March 14, 1856, started the NY&E's interest in this territory. The B&B was planned to connect the NY&E at Carrollton with the Sunbury & Erie and Allegheny Valley railroads near Johnsonburg, Pa., but no construction was complete at the time of its merger with the Buffalo & Pittsburgh Railroad Company on March 22, 1859 to form The Buffalo, Bradford & Pittsburgh Railroad Company (BB&P). The BB&P was leased to the Erie Railway from January 1, 1866. Ultimately the BB&P and several small affiliates (combined with 49.9 miles of trackage rights over the neighboring Buffalo, Rochester & Pittsburgh Railroad) formed the Erie's Bradford Division.

The next major portion of what became the Mahoning Division dates to February 22, 1848, with the incorporation in Ohio of The Cleveland & Mahoning Railroad Company (C&M). In 1856, the C&M opened a single-track railroad, built to Ohio's unique 4'10" gauge (thus "Ohio Gauge"), from Cleveland to Youngstown, OH. The C&M was the first railroad to serve Youngstown and the Mahoning Valley, then on the verge of its transformation to a steel-making and manufacturing center. Capitalizing on the growing demand for coal, C&M interests assisted in the formation and construction of two coal-focused railroads. The first, the Liberty & Vienna Railroad Company (L&V), was incorporated December 7, 1868, and opened an Ohio Gauge line from Vienna Junction (Near Mosier) to Liberty, OH in 1870. On April 24, 1869, the second was incorporated, the Niles & New Lisbon Railway Company (N&NL), which opened a 35.5-mile line between its Ohio namesakes in 1870. In 1861 the C&M had also extended its line from Youngstown to Hazelton, OH and in 1865 from Youngstown to the Ohio-Pennsylvania State Line. On October 7, 1863, the C&M was leased to the Atlantic & Great Western Railway Company (A&GW). August 14, 1872, saw the C&M merged with its two affiliates (L&V and N&NL) to form The Cleveland & Mahoning Valley Railway Company (C&MV). On the same date, the C&MV was leased to the A&GW. With its 1863 lease of the C&M, the A&GW established the first Mahoning Division to administer the leased property—it was a name that would shine in railroad circles for more than 113 years.

The presence of the Erie Lackawanna in Ohio was the dream of two men. In Franklin Mills, OH, a small community on the banks of the Cuyahoga River in Portage County, Marvin Kent, scion of a local entrepreneur, and himself a savvy businessman, saw with envy the growing prosperity of nearby Ravenna, county seat and a station on the newly-completed (in 1852) Cleveland & Pittsburgh Railroad (ultimately a leased line of the Pennsylvania Railroad system). During the C&P's construction, Kent tried unsuccessfully to induce it to build a short (3-mile) branch into Franklin Mills, but he was refused. Having failed at getting the 3-mile road built, Kent optimistically decided to build a 300-mile trans-Ohio railroad and on March 10, 1851, caused the incorporation of the Franklin & Warren Railroad. His goal was to provide the New York & Erie an outlet to the west.

Unfortunately the Commonwealth of Pennsylvania was an effective barrier to reaching New York State. In those ante-bellum days, Pennsylvania leaders wanted the commerce of Ohio and the west to reach Tidewater at Philadelphia, thereby traversing the length of the Commonwealth. Kent and his Ohio supporters were able to find allies in Meadville, Pa., where William Reynolds, a local lawyer-businessman, also shared Kent's vision to place his community on a main line to the west. Reynolds and his supporters incorporated the Meadville Railroad Company on May 20, 1857, with an expansive charter to construct and operate a railroad from Meadville to almost anywhere in Pennsylvania.

Demonstrating their increasing alliance, Kent's Franklin & Warren Railroad Company changed its name to the Atlantic & Great Western Railway Company (of Ohio) on January 1, 1856. Reynold's Meadville Railroad Company, in turn, changed its name to the Atlantic & Great Western Railway Company (of Pennsylvania) on April 15, 1858.

[1] As of December 31, 1975
[2] Buffalo (latterly Buffalo Terminal), Mahoning, Marion, New York, Scranton, and Susquehanna Divisions
[3] "Official List of Open & Prepay Stations Number 72," effective April 15, 1957

Kent and Reynolds both recognized that the NY&E (and later its successor, the Erie Railway) was dissatisfied with its western terminal at Dunkirk, N.Y. Capitalizing on this, they saw the possibilities of a railroad linking the NY&E with the Ohio River at Cincinnati, then the leading city of the West. Cincinnati was also the eastern terminus of the Ohio & Mississippi Railroad, whose broad-gauge (6-foot) line had in 1857 reached west to the Mississippi River at East St. Louis, Ill. In 1859 the three separate Atlantic & Great Western Railways (by then there was one incorporated in each New York, Ohio, and Pennsylvania) formed what we would now term a joint venture to construct and operate a broad-gauge railroad from a connection with the NY&E at Salamanca, N.Y., to Dayton, OH, a distance of 388.3 miles. Unlike the NY&E whose original 447.8-mile Piermont-Dunkirk, N.Y. Main Line required 19 years to complete, the A&GW route was completed on June 21, 1864, less than five years after its commencement. That there was financial power behind the A&GW was evident since it was completed in the midst of the most destructive war the United States had ever been engaged in.

Initially, the A&GW was organized with five divisions: the First (Salamanca to Meadville), the Second (Meadville to Kent), the Third (Kent to Galion), the Fourth (Galion to Dayton), and the Mahoning (Cleveland to Pymatuning Junction and branches). In 1865 the A&GW built in its own name, the Franklin Branch, consisting of a broad-gauge railroad from Buchanan Junction (near Meadville) to Franklin, Pa., which was 25 miles. By 1871 the Franklin Branch had been extended to Oil City, Pa., another 8.9 miles.

Jamestown, N.Y., at the south end of Chautauqua Lake in southwestern New York State, blossomed with the August 25, 1860 opening of the A&GW. On March 23, 1872, demand for a connection between this emerging commercial center and the region's Queen City, Buffalo, resulted in the incorporation of The Buffalo & Jamestown Railroad Company (B&J). Construction proceeded slowly with completion—and bankruptcy—in 1877. The Buffalo & South Western Rail Road Company (B&SW) was incorporated December 11, 1877, and the next day it acquired the B&J's property, a railroad from Buffalo to Jamestown, 67.8 miles. The B&SW was operated as an independent railroad until July 31, 1880, when it was leased to the New York, Lake Erie & Western Railroad Company. Under NYLE&W control the B&SW was operated as a part of the Buffalo Division.

The last major Nineteenth Century addition to what became the modern Mahoning Division's main line had its roots in the July 16, 1873 incorporation of the Sharon Railway that in August 1876 completed a railroad from Clarksville (later renamed Transfer), PA to Sharon where trains continued over the 2.1-mile Westerman Coal & Iron Railroad (a privately-owned railroad leased by the Erie Railway from April 1, 1868) to the Mahoning Division at State Line. With the completion of the Sharon Railway, the A&GW was able to operate trains, especially through passenger trains, via Youngstown and the Mahoning Valley.

Rounding out principal Nineteenth Century lines forming the Mahoning Division was the 1888-89 completion of The New Castle & Shenango Valley Railroad Company's (NC&SV) 16.7-mile line from West Middlesex to New Castle, PA. The NC&SV was the extension of the Sharon Railway's Sharon-West Middlesex, PA branch that was built circa 1876.

After 1868 the A&GW and its successors were leased to (with some minor breaks) and operated by the Erie Railway and its own successors. The traffic focus in this period was still on the Cincinnati gateway. Operating divisions paralleled engine crew operating districts, generally being 100 miles or less in length.

The June 17, 1883 opening of the Chicago & Atlantic Railway between Marion, OH, and Hammond, IN. (with Trackage Rights beyond to Chicago's Dearborn Station) transformed the future Mahoning Division. With the opening of service to Chicago, the New York, Lake Erie & Western Railroad, which operated the railroad between Jersey City, N.J., and Dayton, OH, became a major player in the so-called "Trunk Line" (i.e., Chicago to the Eastern Seaboard) world.

It quickly developed that the tracks between Hornell, NY and Marion, OH became a major barrier to developing the NYLE&W into an efficient and profitable railroad. Most of the Hornell-Marion line was single-track with an insufficient number of passing sidings. Further, the grade profile between Hornell and Marion severely restricted freight train size.

While double-tracking slowly progressed through the 1880's and 1890's the NYLE&W's financial position was weak. The nationwide financial Panic of 1893 forced it into bankruptcy and it emerged in 1895 as the Erie Railroad. By 1900 new financial arrangements and a dynamic new leadership under President Frederick D. Underwood focused on making the Erie a true heavy-duty railroad. In addition to heavier rail, the Underwood Administration completed much double-tracking and, in one case, an innovative arrangement with the Bessemer & Lake Erie Railroad (B&LE), permitting a number of Erie trains to use the B&LE between Meadville and Shenango, distantly paralleling a single-track stretch of Erie track. More importantly, arrangements were made for two lengthy new lines, which increased capacity and significantly reduced grades.

To provide additional track capacity and reduce grades on the Meadville Division, the A&GW's former First Division, the Columbus & Erie Railroad Company, was incorporated September 5, 1905 to construct and operate a single-track railroad from Niobe Junction, N.Y. to near Columbus, Pa., a distance of 13.02 miles. The line opened in December 1908 and, in connection with grade reduction improvements from Lakewood, NY, to State Line, did much to improve train movement on the Meadville Division.

The line from Hornell to Salamanca, by the turn of the century a key part of the Allegany Division (originally the NY&E's Western Division), forced trains to surmount two significant summits in Allegany County, NY: Cuba Summit at MP JC 377.5 (reached by 1.07% grades eastbound and 1.05% grades westbound) and the aptly-named Tip Top at MP JC 344.3 (reached by 0.78% grades eastbound and a 13-mile 1.05% grade westbound). Combine these grades with a mostly single-track line and add in a touch of winter and moving trains became a major challenge.

Underwood decided to literally outflank the problem by incorporating the Genesee River Railroad Company on August 21, 1905 to construct and operate a 33.2-mile railroad from Cuba Junction, N.Y., MP JC 383.9 on the Allegany Division, northeast to River Junction, NY, MP JC 358.1 on the Buffalo Division. In contrast to the grade-plagued line over Cuba Summit and Tip Top the Genesee River Railroad had no westbound grade exceeding 0.3% or 0.2% eastbound.

It took Frederick Underwood's successor, John J. Bernet, to pull the Mahoning Division into its peak steam era performance. With even more heavy rail and bridge strengthening, Bernet introduced the Erie's iconic S-class Berkshire-type (2-8-4 wheel arrangement) steam locomotive to fast freight train service. The Erie, heretofore somewhat of a drag freight-era railroad, entered the Depression as a true fast freight railroad. Much of that reputation was earned by fast, on-time performance on the Mahoning Division.

On the eve of the Depression, June 2, 1929, the Erie introduced its premier New York-Chicago passenger trains, appropriately #1 and #2, the *Erie Limited*. For Mahoning Division patrons it provided a convenient, comfortable daylight train in both directions between New York and Youngstown and excellent overnight service between Youngstown and Chicago.

The Depression ultimately caused the bankruptcy, on January 19, 1938, of the Erie Railroad Company. It emerged from bankruptcy on December 22, 1941, rather quickly and, in retrospect, without as much a debt-reducing "haircut" as might have been done. The "new" Erie had a massive wartime job. For the Mahoning Division the task was especially challenging as the steel mills of Youngstown and Mahoning Valley became the "Forge of Democracy," turning out steel for the weapons of war while the Main Line saw unprecedented waves of freight and passengers.

The Mahoning Division's sawtooth profile had never been fully corrected despite the new construction of the early Twentieth Century. Because of this, its movement of freight trains even with modern S-class Berkshires was increasingly constrictive. The Bernet Administration had focused on one Berkshire pulling a 5,000-ton train from Chicago to Jersey City, albeit with the help of pushers over Gulf Summit east of Susquehanna, Pa. The broken profile of the railroad between Marion and Meadville forced even the Berkshires to reduce their tonnage to 3,000 tons between these points. The solution required the convergence of wartime necessity and industrial inventiveness in the form of the Erie's first diesel-electric locomotives for road freight service. Acquired from General Motor's Electro-Motive Division in 1944 the six 5,400-h.p. locomotives (as the Erie characterized them) were actually 12 "A" and 12 "B" units acquired at a cost of $3 million (plus another $1 million for a diesel shop in Marion, OH). These locomotives, however, almost single-handedly broke the tonnage restriction of the sawtooth grades between Marion and Meadville. Eighteen Berkshires were released for urgent service on other parts of the Erie system by the new diesels. More so, these diesels made the Erie a believer in diesel-electric locomotives leading to its early (1951) main line dieselization (steam stayed in New Jersey suburban service until 1953).

With the coming of peace in 1945 the lines that would become the modern Mahoning Division were organized as two divisions: the Allegany, Bradford, Meadville, and B&SW Division was headquartered at Salamanca while the Mahoning Division was headquartered at Youngstown. The Mahoning Division, in turn, was organized as the First Subdivision (Cleveland to Pymatuning, via Youngstown, and the Lisbon Branch and New Castle Branch) and the Second Subdivision (Meadville to Kent via Latimer and the Franklin Branch).

From the 1920's the Erie had organized itself into Districts, which ultimately came down to two: the Eastern District with a General Manager and staff based at Jersey City overseeing the operation of the Divisions east of Buffalo and Hornell (both inclusive) and the Western District with a General Manager and staff based at Youngstown overseeing the Divisions west of Buffalo and Hornell (both exclusive).

The last major pre-merger new track construction on the Mahoning Division was the construction of 4,628 feet of new track in 1948-49 to permit the Erie's newly dieselized Cleveland passenger service to operate into Cleveland Union Terminal.

The merger of The Delaware, Lackawanna & Western Railroad Company into the Erie Railroad Company to form the Erie-Lackawanna Railroad Company on October 17, 1960 made little initial change in the pre-merger arrangement of Western District divisions. It did have the effect of increasing through freight traffic as the merged EL began to take as long a haul on former DL&W traffic as possible. All of this increased traffic on the Mahoning Division. Unfortunately, the new EL was unable to attain profitability and suffered record losses in 1962. It came as no surprise that the District arrangement was abolished that year and the Allegany, Bradford, Meadville, and B&SW Division was aborted and its territory and functions taken over by an expanded Mahoning Division.

In its final 1962-1976 EL format the Mahoning Division consisted of the following:

	Miles
Main Line:	
Hornell, N.Y., to Brady Lake, O., via Bear Lake and Latimer	269.2
Columbus & Erie RR:	
NE Junction, N.Y., to CM Junction, Pa.	13.2
River Line:	
River Junction to CB Junction, N.Y.	32.6
1st Subdivision:	
Cleveland (Riverbed Yard) to Pymatuning, Pa.	87.9
Buffalo & Southwestern Branch:	
Buffalo to Waterboro, N.Y.	58.6
Hidi Spur:	
at Gowanda, N.Y.	1.2
Dunkirk Branch:	
WC Junction to Dunkirk, N.Y.	45.5
Bradford Branch:	
Carrollton, N.Y., to Lewis Run, Pa.	17.2
Toby Branch:	
WI Tower to Hydes, Pa.	7.6
Oil City-Franklin Branch:	
Buchanan to Oil City, Pa.	33.3
New Castle Branch:	
New Castle (Gardner Avenue) to Ferrona, Pa.	23.4
Lisbon Branch:	
Niles to Lisbon, O.	33.2
Haselton Branch:	
Youngstown to Haselton, O.	1.6
Canal Branch:	
Youngstown to Girard, O.	7.0
CUT Connection:	
CUT Switch to Cleveland (Broadway), O.	1.4
Trackage Rights over Baltimore & Ohio RR:	
Limestone to Brockway, Pa.	75.6
Total	**708.6**

The post-1962 Mahoning Division was managed from the Terminal Building in Youngstown, which housed the passenger station on its ground floor with Dispatchers, division officers, and staff throughout its five upper stories. Youngstown was the headquarters for the Division Superintendent, an Assistant Superintendent, Master Mechanic, Division Engineer, and a Trainmaster. Trainmasters were also located in Cleveland, OH; Salamanca, NY; and Meadville, PA.; with Track Supervisors at Cuba and Jamestown, NY; Greenville, PA.; and Youngstown, OH. The field supervisory force was remarkably thin, reflecting the professionalism of the EL's rank-and-file employees and greatly improved communications.

Passenger Service at its EL peak consisted of the Hoboken-Chicago service and Pittsburgh-Youngstown-Cleveland service operated in conjunction with the Pittsburgh & Lake Erie Railroad. A look at a typical weekday's First Class Trains arriving and leaving Youngstown in the early EL era[4] is instructive:

12:59 AM . #11 originate and depart for Chicago
4:40 AM . #2 arrive from Chicago
5:04 AM . #2 depart for Hoboken
6:00 AM . #629 originate and depart for Cleveland
7:15 AM . #8 arrive from Chicago
7:25 AM . #8 depart for Hoboken
9:15 AM . #5 arrive from Hoboken
9:20 AM . #5 depart for Chicago
9:40 AM . #624 arrive from Cleveland—becomes P&LE #274
9:48 AM . P&LE 274 depart for Pittsburgh
10:00 AM . #625 originate and depart for Cleveland
11:25 AM . #12 arrive and terminate from Chicago
3:41 PM . #7 arrive from Hoboken
3:57 PM . #7 depart for Chicago
7:10 PM . #628 arrives from Cleveland
7:30 PM . P&LE 273 arrive from Pittsburgh—becomes EL #623
7:35 PM . #623 depart for Cleveland
7:47 PM . #6 arrive from Chicago
8:00 PM . #6 depart for Hoboken
11:10 PM . #686 arrive from Cleveland
11:44 PM . #1 arrive from Hoboken
11:59 PM . #1 depart for Chicago

As impressive as the Mahoning Division's passenger operations were, it was a Division built and operated for freight. In 1965, yard crews were on duty at 16 locations and at least 13 local freight trains were dispatched from 10 locations, in addition to extra freight trains and such exotica as Hot Metal shuttles between Youngstown and Sharon, Hubbard and Warren. On a typical day towards the end of the EL one might see the following Symbol Through Freights pass "SN" Tower[5], the crossing of the First Subdivision (Cleveland to Pymatuning) and the Second Subdivision (Meadville to Brady Lake [Kent]):

First Trick
NE-97 Maybrook to Marion
TC-99 Binghamton to Marion
#78 Chicago to Meadville via Brier Hill
TC-100 Chicago to Binghamton
PB-100 Chicago to Binghamton
NY-100 Chicago to Croxton

Second Trick
MC-1 Meadville to Cleveland
NY-97 Croxton to Marion
BM-7 Buffalo to Marion via Brier Hill (Youngstown)
NY-99 Croxton to Chicago
Advance CX-99 Croxton to Chicago
PB-99 Binghamton to Chicago
CX-99 Croxton to Chicago
2nd NY-100 Chicago to Croxton
#62 Marion to Cleveland (ran around train at Leavittsburg)
#92 Marion to Meadville via Brier Hill (Youngstown)
PN-98 Chicago to Scranton
NY-98 Chicago to Croxton

Third Trick
#61 Cleveland to Kent (ran around train at Leavittsburg)
MC-3 Meadville to Marion via Brier Hill (Youngstown)
BM-9 Buffalo to Marion
MF-74 Chicago to Buffalo via Brier Hill (Youngstown)
NE-74 Chicago to Maybrook
NY-74 Marion to Croxton
CM-2 Cleveland to Meadville via Brier Hill (Youngstown)

Alas, despite this sea of traffic the EL was unable to survive. A final flood-precipitated bankruptcy in June 1972 and ultimately much of the EL and the Mahoning Division was absorbed into Conrail on April 1, 1976. For a time the Mahoning Division survived, shorn of much of its through traffic, and unable to cope with the post-Conrail devastation of the Youngstown and Mahoning Valley steel industry. On October 30, 1977, Conrail merged its Mahoning Division with the Valley Division (a former Penn Central Division also headquartered in Youngstown) to form the Youngstown Division. This brought to an end 114 years of Mahoning Division existence, leaving a legacy through the decades of excellent railroad performance in densely trafficked territory.

For devotees of the Mahoning Division the Conrail era brought little to cheer about. The former Erie Lackawanna was not a good fit into the Conrail system and while it arguably could have survived outside Conrail, it was never given that chance. For the former Mahoning Division, abandonment or placing long segments of track out-of-service seemed to be its fate. But the emergence of some entrepreneurial railroaders from the mold of Marvin Kent and William Reynolds together with the fortuitous split of Conrail in 1999 between Conrail and Norfolk Southern have brought life back to many miles of Mahoning Division track. The story of the Mahoning Division's near-death experience under Conrail and its new post-Conrail life is, however, a work in progress. For now, join us in looking at *Erie Lackawanna In Color, Volume 7: Mahoning Division* by Stephen M. Timko, when the Mahoning Division was the economic heart of the Erie and Erie Lackawanna Railroads.

Michael J. Connor
April 18, 2011

---

[4] Per Mahoning Division Timetable #68, effective October 29, 1961
[5] Per Scranton Division-Susquehanna Division-Buffalo Terminal Division-Mahoning Division-Marion Division Timetable #4, effective February 24, 1974

ERIE LACKAWANNA RAILWAY

SUMMARY OF LOCOMOTIVES
AS OF MARCH 31, 1976

NUMBER SERIES	MODEL	BUILDER	HP
362-371	SW-8	GM-EMD	800
401-402	NW-2	EMC	1000
404-427, 441-445	NW-2	GM-EMD	1000
428-433	SW-7	GM-EMD	1200
434-440, 446-455	SW-9	GM-EMD	1200
456-463	SW-1200	GM-EMD	1200
520-521, 532, 539, 542	S-2	Alco	1000
526	S-4	Alco	1000
809-810, 812-822, 824-833	E8a	GM-EMD	2250
903-907, 909-910, 912-913, 953-954	RS-2	Alco	1500
914-918, 920-928, 930-933	RS-3	Alco	1600
1004	RS-3	Alco/EL	1600
1005-1010, 1013-1026, 1028-1029, 1033-1056	RS-3	Alco	1600
1057, 1060	RS-3m	Alco/EL	1125
1200-1246, 1270-1284, 1400-1401, 1403-1409	GP-7	GM-EMD	1500
1260-1265	GP-9	GM-EMD	1750
2401-2415	C-424	Alco	2400
2451-2462	C-425	Alco	2500
2501-2527	U25b	GE	2500
2551-2586	GP-35	GM-EMD	2500
3301-3315	U-33c	GE	3300
3316-3328	U-36c	GE	3600
3601-3634	SD-45	GM-EMD	3600
3635-3636, 3638-3668	SDP-45	GM-EMD	3600
3669-3681	SD-45-2	GM-EMD	3600
6321, 6331, 6341, 6351, 6361	F7a	GM-EMD	1500
6112, 6322, 6332, 6342, 6352, 6362	F7b	GM-EMD	1500
7091, 7094, 7101, 7104, 7111, 7114, 7121, 7124, 7131, 7134	F7a	GM-EMD	1500
7092, 7093, 7102, 7103, 7112, 7113, 7122, 7123, 7133	F7b	GM-EMD	1500

Note: The Erie Lackawanna locomotive fleet was very complex with the renumbering of units in 1960 to fit into the new railroad's proper classification sequence. Additionally, many model Alco and EMD carbody type locomotives were traded in on second generation locomotive purchases. Early Alco and EMD switchers were purged from the roster shortly after the Erie-DL&W merger and FM, Lima and Baldwin units disappeared from the roster during the late 1960s. This is not to be considered a locomotive roster, but rather a summary of locomotives.

TABLE OF CONTENTS

THE CLEVELAND RIVERBED 10
CLEVELAND 18
NORTH RANDALL 28
SOLON TO LEAVITTSBURG 30
LEAVITTSBURG 32
THE MAHONING VALLEY 34
THE SHENANGO VALLEY 54
KENT TO MEADVILLE VIA 2ND SUB-DIVISION 55
MEADVILLE 64
MEADVILLE TO SALAMANCA AND THE B&SW BRANCH 72
SALAMANCA TO HORNELL INCLUDING DUNKIRK AND BRADFORD BRANCHES . . 108
BUFFALO 117
THE MAHONING DIVISION POST EL 118

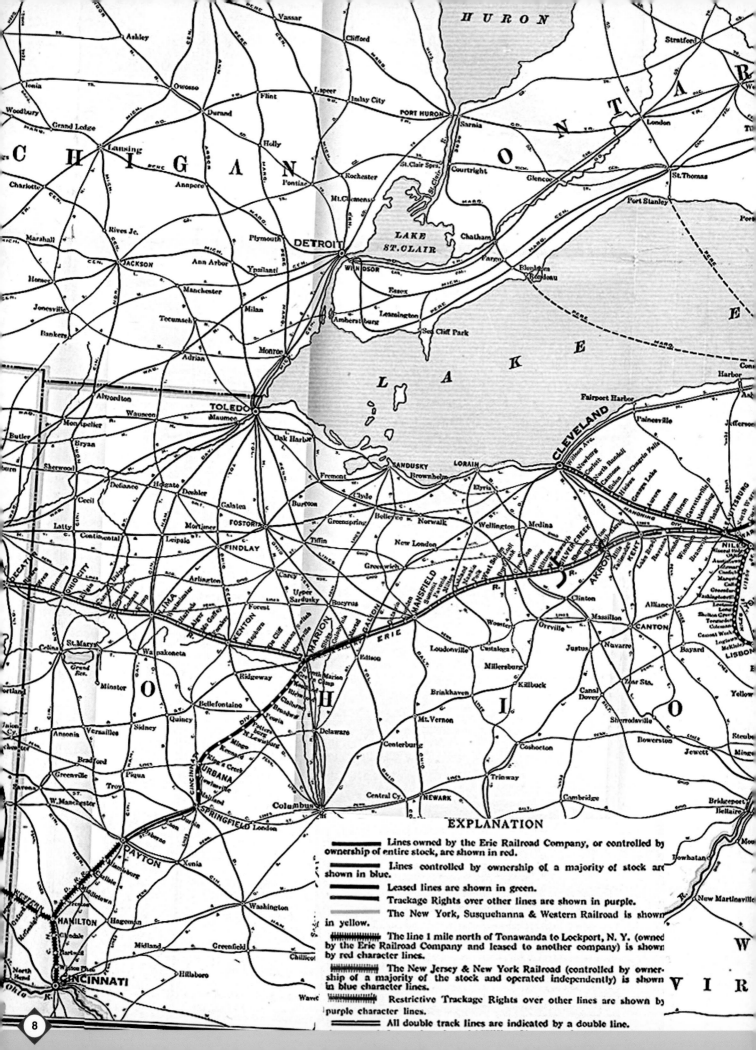

EXPLANATION

Lines owned by the Erie Railroad Company, or controlled by ownership of entire stock, are shown in red.

Lines controlled by ownership of a majority of stock are shown in blue.

Leased lines are shown in green.

Trackage Rights over other lines are shown in purple.

The New York, Susquehanna & Western Railroad is shown in yellow.

The line 1 mile north of Tonawanda to Lockport, N. Y. (owned by the Erie Railroad Company and leased to another company) is shown by red character lines.

The New Jersey & New York Railroad (controlled by ownership of a majority of the stock and operated independently) is shown in blue character lines.

Restrictive Trackage Rights over other lines are shown by purple character lines.

All double track lines are indicated by a double line.

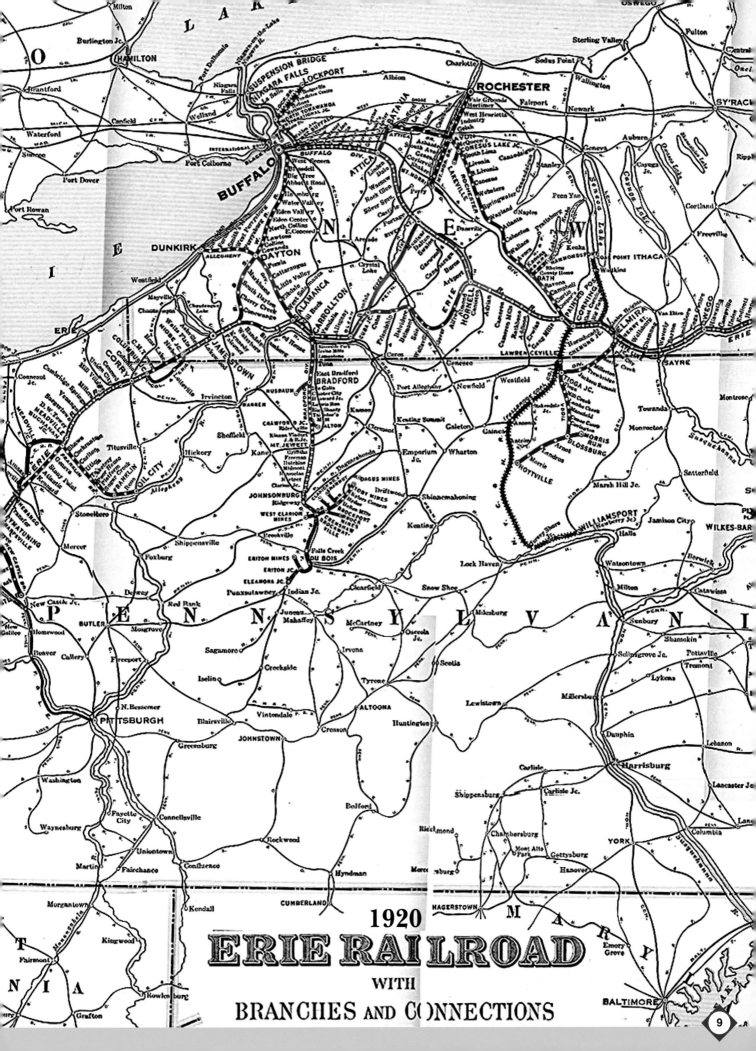

1920
ERIE RAILROAD
WITH
BRANCHES AND CONNECTIONS

The River Bed was the beginning of the 1st Sub-Division, located on the Cuyahoga River in Cleveland. Most of the actual River Bed Yard and the dock operation was actually located at a minus MP 0 location. The River Bed operations consisted of a yard office, manned when boats were to unload, and usually only between April and Thanksgiving. In addition, the Huletts, the side-arm pusher units and the dock maintenance offices made up the River Bed complex. The portion of railroad known as the River Bed was a double tracked line, void of signals, and operated on verbal permission of the operator at Bridge 2.22 near Broadway Avenue.

It was a very slow-speed railroad with trains moving at nearly a walking pace. It was normal to have several crews working at the River Bed at one time when boats were unloading. The River Bed Yard Job was supplied with empty hoppers from Drag Downs and the loaded trains departed in cuts of 55 cars of ore on Drag Ups. Drag Downs and Drag Ups were names assigned to the shuttle service between the River Bed and North Randall and were manned by Cleveland crews. Youngstown crews occasionally operated to the River Bed for a cut of 55 cars of ore to fill out with 55 more at North Randall and return to Youngstown.

ABOVE • GP35 #2576 is utilized as the Riverbed Yard Engine in this November 1975 photo. The Huletts are ready and several of the EL's 70-ton "gold stripe" hoppers are in position for loading. During 1975 the EL's dock moved 8.44% of all ore loaded in Cleveland vs. 11.15% in 1974. The 1975 loadings produced 17,210 revenue carloads vs. 26,964 in the previous year. *(Mike Kopach, ELHS Archives Collection)*

RIGHT, TOP • Another GP35, this time #2556, toils in the River Bed as a U36c and a U33c depart on a Drag-Up in December 1975. "Drag Up" trains were utilized to haul 55 cars of ore the dozen miles to North Randall over grades reaching 1.79%. At North Randall a Randall Turn would arrive from Youngstown with empty hoppers and gather two cuts of ore to return to the hungry blast furnaces of the Mahoning and Shenango Valleys. *(Mike Kopach, ELHS Archives Collection)*

RIGHT, BOTTOM • U25b #2514 has drawn the assignment for the River Bed Yard Job in this January 1975 photo. Many ore dumpers could not accommodate 100-ton hoppers on account of their being either too heavy or too tall so the task of hauling ore fell to the 70-ton hoppers. Both EL and P&LE supplied hoppers for trains destined to the P&LE RR. In this scene, some Pittsburg & Shawmut hoppers have filtered into the ore pool; it wasn't unusual to see cars from foreign roads on occasion. *(Mike Kopach, ELHS Archives Collection)*

ABOVE • The steamer *Champlain* is "working" at the River Bed Dock in November 1973. GE U25b #2507 is assigned to the River Bed Yard Job handling the loaded cars from the loading tracks after the Huletts load the cars. The Cleveland Union Terminal, a complex containing a department store, hotel and an office tower, can be seen to the right. The Erie Lackawanna's system headquarters were located in the complex's Midland, Guildhall, and Republic Buildings. *(Mike Kopach, ELHS Archives Collection)*

LEFT • A crewmember walks from the River Bed Yard Office on River Street to the GP35 to make a move in the yard toward the end of the 1975 shipping season. This would be the dock's final year with Conrail arriving in April and the dock operations moving to Whiskey Island. GP35 #2576 is seen in its as-delivered paint scheme with the maroon letters above the band. A revised paint scheme placed yellow letters inside the maroon band, a much more attractive arrangement.

(Mike Kopach, ELHS Archives Collection)

RIGHT • Newly painted caboose C-178 is seen near the River Bed Yard Office in the fall of 1974.

(Mike Kopach, ELHS Archives Collection)

RIGHT • A westbound empty hopper train passes a loaded ore train in "the tunnels" between HD Yard and the River Bed Yard in June 1974. Certain classes of locomotives were prohibited from passing in the tunnels and it was up to the operator at Bridge 2.22 to make certain that an incident did not occur. *(Mike Kopach, ELHS Archives Collection)*

ABOVE • The colors of U25b #2523 and the River Bed Yard Office add a splash of brilliance to an otherwise dreary surrounding in December 1975. *(Mike Kopach, ELHS Archives Collection)*

BELOW • A Drag Up crew with Alco C425 #2455 and GE U36c #3328 is ready to depart the River Bed for North Randall with a cut of ore on April 21, 1974. Two-unit combinations such as these replaced earlier consists of three FM H24-66 Train Masters on these runs.
(John McCown, ELHS Archives Collection)

ABOVE • A highway lift bridge forms the backdrop for this great photo of the "One-double O-Seven" switching the River Bed in February 1975. Ore season was about to begin and a 25-year-old Alco was filling the empty yard with hoppers in anticipation of the first boat. This year would be the final year for the EL's River Bed dock. *(Mike Kopach, ELHS Archives Collection)*

BELOW • The Erie Dock Company was a ghostly looking place in this February 1976 photo. The River Bed Yard Office is along the fence at the left near River Street road crossing. The entire yard is void of railcars, save for one Structures Department camp car, and only one vehicle is in the parking lot. With the coming of Conrail in two months, the boats would be shifted to the former PC dock at Whiskey Island and this property would be placed for sale. *(Mike Kopach, ELHS Archives Collection)*

ABOVE • It's the winter of 1975-1976 and a lone Alco RS3 can be seen across the Cuyahoga River as it works the River Bed Yard Job. The Huletts are seen in action unloading what could be the final boat for the NYP&O Dock. *(Mike Kopach, ELHS Archives Collection)*

ORE UNLOADED AT THE NYP&O (RIVER BED) DOCKS FOR 1975, THE FINAL YEAR OF OPERATION:

CONSIGNEE	LOCATION	CARS	TONS
Detroit Steel Company	Portsmouth, OH	513	36,599
Jones & Laughlin Steel Company	Aliquippa, PA	1,503	105,187
Republic Steel Corporation	Warren, OH	3,985	299,347
Republic Steel Corporation	Youngstown, OH	1,343	100,694
Sharon Steel Corporation	Farrell (Sharon), PA	1,119	79,653
Shenango, Incorporated	Neville Island, PA	2,856	214,306
Youngstown Sheet & Tube Company	Brier Hill Works, OH	687	51,513
Youngstown Sheet & Tube Company	Campbell Works, OH	4,939	352,421
Wheeling-Pittsburgh Steel Company	Monessen, PA	2,039	153,074
TOTAL		**18,984**	**1,392,794**

ABOVE • This April 1979 view of the River Bed Yard and Erie Dock Company indicates no activity. Steamer *Raymond H. Reiss* of The Cleveland-Cliffs Steamship Company is in winter lay-up at the dock.

Under the Huletts and between the loading tracks ran a narrow-gauge railway with home-built electrically powered side-arm pusher locomotives for positioning cars for loading.

(Mike Kopach, ELHS Archives Collection)

The Cleveland area operations of the Erie Lackawanna Railroad originally centered around HD Yard located at Literary Street west of Bridge 2.22. As the LCL and cross-dock service came to an end in the late 1960s, the Scranton Road Freight House located west of HD Yard was reduced to a billing center. Around that same time, HD Yard was virtually closed as a manned location and the hub of activity was relocated to East 55th Street Yard, also known as "the Avenue." The Avenue housed the Trainmaster, Yardmaster, clerks as well as support track, signal and car department personnel. The locomotive servicing area was north of the yard office and was known as SQ Diesel Shop. A small-scale piggyback ramp operation was also located at the Avenue. East of E55th Street the double track line crossed the four-track PRR line and then curved to the right near Aetna Road where the EL met the stiffest part of the 1.79% ascending grade between the River Bed and North Randall. Aetna Road was also the location of an important interchange with the Newburgh & South Shore Railroad. If that wasn't enough activity in a confined area, the EL was the route used by the N&W to connect the former NKP and W&LE railroads. W&LE and NKP "pullers" operated back and forth between those roads making several trips per day. A similar arrangement permitted the NKP to access the PRR via Erie Lackawanna trackage.

BELOW • Being the sole surviving passenger train in a large terminal is costly. In earlier days Erie Lackawanna trains arriving in Cleveland's Union Terminal would cut the engine off and return to SQ Diesel Shop at E. 55th Street, leaving the train to be cleaned, serviced and inspected by CUT personnel. In later years, in order to reduce both the costs of those services as well as hourly storage charges, the crew backed the train to SQ Shop where EL forces cleaned and serviced the train, turned the locomotive and stored it until required in the afternoon. In this October 1976 photo we see the train at E. 55th Street awaiting return to the terminal while the unit gets a spin on the table. The train is hauled by E8a #833 – the highest road number of the 1951 purchases of this model by DL&W and Erie.

(Mike Kopach, ELHS Archives Collection)

ABOVE • A pair of second-generation units, GP35 #2572 and U25b #2516, waits for assignment at HD Yard near Literary Street in Cleveland in March 1976. The 2500 HP units both originated in the second order for these models from EMD and GE, respectively.

(Mike Kopach, ELHS Archives Collection)

BELOW • When this photo was taken in February 1974, East 55th Street Station was the main yard office for the Cleveland area. The River Bed was "manned" when ore boats were docked and Literary Street was used on occasion. The "Avenue" also doubled as a passenger station for Trains #28 & 29. The New Erie Café is across the street and has been mentioned in other Morning Sun Books. Additionally, models of the café have been noted at ELHS functions.

(Mike Kopach, ELHS Archives Collection)

ABOVE • Train #28 departs Cleveland Union Terminal in the spring of 1975. By this time the train is the last to call at this stately building. The electrified lines to the right are those of the Cleveland Transit System and the Shaker Heights Rapid Transit that merged to become the Cleveland RTA. The weed infested tracks in the foreground are all out of service, save for the one track used for this move.

(Mike Kopach, ELHS Archives Collection)

ABOVE • A year later, #28 departs CUT with three lightweight coaches trailing a single E8 locomotive. Careful viewing of the coaches indicates a substantial passenger load; that's because the train has yet to make its first stop. *(Mike Kopach, ELHS Archives Collection)*

ABOVE • Spring of 1977 has found the Scranton Road Freight House vacated and posted for sale. Less-than-Car-Load (LCL) service ended a score of years prior and billing has been centralized at the new company's Collinwood Yard, thus another ex-Erie property has been declared surplus. The building sets in the shadow of the stately Cleveland Union Terminal complex.

(Mike Kopach, ELHS Archives Collection)

ABOVE • Downgraded to Maintenance-of-Way service and carrying #488001, a former Railway Express Agency car is seen at East 55th Street in Cleveland in November 1977.
(Mike Kopach, ELHS Archives Collection)

ABOVE • Another relic of the high-speed passenger days, M-of-W car #489023 is used as a tool and material storage car in November 1975 at "the Avenue." *(Mike Kopach, ELHS Archives Collection)*

LEFT • Conrail has arrived, as attested by this March 1979 photo that shows a former Penn Central F unit in the distance. Two Erie Lackawanna covered hoppers provide the sanding facilities for the locomotives in this photo.
(Mike Kopach, ELHS Archives Collection)

ABOVE • The EL had a healthy industrial base in Cleveland with many major industries producing chemical products that required inbound raw materials.

The original EL U25b, #2501 is seen doing industrial switching at HD Yard in May 1975. *(Mike Kopach, ELHS Archives Collection)*

ABOVE • Alco C424 #2408 hauls a cut of empty P&LE hoppers out of the Standard Oil Company refinery in September 1976. The rear of the train has just cleared Broadway Avenue and the train is about to shove east to East 55th Street Yard. The location of the photo is

Bridge 2.22, where the operator was also the bridge tender. US Steel's Central Furnace stands in the background. The weeds growing in the track are testament to the fact that the River Bed Ore Dock was not used after April 1, 1976. *(Mike Kopach, ELHS Archives Collection)*

LEFT • Another view of industrial switching in Cleveland, this time with Alco C424 #2414 doing the honors. Note the horn placement over the engineer's windshield in this summer 1976 photo. This modification was made to allow clearance through "the tunnels" between HD Yard and the River Bed.   *(Mike Kopach, ELHS Archives Collection)*

BELOW • There's a dusting of snow on the ground in this January 1975 view of SD45 #3608 and SDP-45 #3646 at HD Yard. It's a little late in the season for an ore train but we know of no other reason for a crew to be using this big power and shoving a caboose toward the River Bed.
                (Mike Kopach, ELHS Archives Collection)

ABOVE • A former DL&W troop sleeper, now assigned to Carpenter Gang EC-77, is seen alongside "The Avenue" yard office at East 55th Street in this March 1979 photo. The car has been "white-lined" as indicated by the white line painted through the number, indicating the car has been retired and will be sold for scrap.
(Mike Kopach, ELHS Archives Collection)

BELOW • Two more former troop sleepers, these from the Erie fleet, repose at East 55th Street in this April 1976 photo. M-of-W #455000 and 455001 are assigned to the Communications Department. *(Mike Kopach, ELHS Archives Collection)*

LEFT • When a Drag Up passed with a cut of ore, one certainly took notice. SD45 #3622 and a six-axle General Electric move 55 loads of taconite pellets past the E55th Street station and yard office in July 1974. The rear of the train should just be clearing the West End Tower interlocking as the head end leans into a three-degree curve. The train has eight additional miles of uphill grade to overcome, the steepest at 1.79% prior to reaching the top at North Randall. The Avenue Yard appears quite busy with general freight, piggyback and M-of-W equipment.
(Ron Rohrbaugh, ELHS Archives Collection)

ABOVE • Train #28 polishes the diamonds of the four-track PC, ex-PRR crossing in this 1971 photo at C&P Tower, or "Erie Crossing," as it was known on the P Company. A Temporary Speed Sign can be seen beside the second coach, indicating a speed restriction was in effect at this location. The tower was demolished in a derailment on February 15, 1977 and the interlocking became remote-controlled from the PRR's Harvard Avenue Tower.

(William F. Herrmann, ELHS Archives Collection)

RIGHT • Here's another view of the well-documented commuter train, this time at East 131st Street and Miles Avenue, locally known as Corlett Crossing. Corlett was the location where the crossing was protected by both a towerman who operated the gates and a groundman who manned a stop sign. Automatic gates were installed in the late fall of 1965, eliminating those two positions. In this November 1971 photo, one of the favored E8s, #816, draws four cars upgrade over the busy intersections. "The next stop is Lee Road, Lee Road, Shaker Heights. This way out please."

(Ron Rohrbaugh, ELHS Archives Collection)

NORTH RANDALL

In pre-Erie Lackawanna days, North Randall was the location of a large ore dock where pellet "dirt ore" was stored for various steel companies. The Ore Dock was a victim of a violent storm in the 1950s as well as improved shipping schedules and service on the great lakes. In EL days, North Randall was the site of a ten-track classification yard on the westbound side where empty hoppers were marshaled prior to being advanced to the River Bed for loading. On the eastbound side, Drag Ups would haul iron ore from the River Bed in 55 car cuts and set off in storage tracks known as #1 and #2 Cannons and #1 and #2 Tank for Randall Turns to pick up and move to the hungry furnaces of the Mahoning and Shenango Valleys. Additionally, North Randall was the home to twenty or so rail-served industries. The EL enjoyed a vigorous business of delivering approximately 60 cars per day to these industries. The depot at North Randall employed an Agent-Operator, a clerk and a night Operator-Clerk in the mid-60's, where the newly-hired author held his first "regular" position in the fall of 1965.

ABOVE • Three cabooses, including one behind C-194, sit on the House and Middle Tracks behind the depot at North Randall in the fall of 1976. EL caboose cars, even the newest ones, were heated with coal, thus the pile of coal near the building. The signal to the extreme right of the photo is identified as signal 11-2M and the bottom head is a position light style Telephone Train Order Signal controlled by the Agent-Operator at North Randall. The TTO signals were used only by the Erie and later Erie Lackawanna Railroads and were quickly eliminated by Conrail after a year or two.

(Mike Kopach, ELHS Archives Collection)

BELOW • North Randall Station wasn't much to look at in October 1976 and it was the coldest place I ever worked back in the winter of 1965. Three cabooses are parked behind the station as an Alco C424 and a leased BN, former SP&S RS3, are in the clear in the Pocket Track with their caboose. The only dating feature that indicates Conrail has arrived is the leased locomotive. North Randall was still a passenger stop for Trains #29 and #28 Monday through Friday.

(Mike Kopach, ELHS Archives Collection)

ABOVE • In previous Morning Sun Books we've seen many great photos of #28, the EL's last surviving commuter train outside suburban New Jersey. This photo of Train #28 is from a new vantage point: the bluff just west of the overhead bridge at Warrensville Center Road. The semaphore signals in the background are signals 10-2M (east) displaying Stop & Proceed and 10-1M (west) displaying Proceed. The fireman peers at the photographer as the engineer throttles down and makes a "first service" brake reduction for the stop at North Randall in this June 1974 photo. *(Ron Rohrbaugh, ELHS Archives Collection)*

The double track rail line between a location near Solon and a location near Leavittsburg was reduced to single track in the mid 1960s after the passenger trains were reduced to one in each direction. The Automatic Block Signal System was changed to Absolute Permissive Block with spring switches installed at each end and at a two-mile double track section near Mantua. The 1st Sub-Division line between Solon and Leavittsburg saw the Monday to Friday commuter train, a Cleveland-Meadville train in each direction, a Brier Hill-Cleve-land train in each direction, a local freight that worked from Cleveland or North Randall to Phalanx and return as well as a local from Brier Hill to Phalanx daily. This was in addition to the seasonal ore and empty hopper trains that numbered several in each direction. Solon was the home to several small industries such as Weiss Noodle and others and Geauga Lake, Mantua, Garrettsville-Hiram and Phalanx all had local industries consisting of sand quarries, coal, lumber and feed dealers.

ABOVE • Former Erie RR wooden caboose #04961, privately owned, sets behind the Solon Station in July 1982. After the EL closed the location, the 1902 station was acquired by the N&W for its local agency office for many years. The EL and the N&W (NKP) crossed at Solon at an automatic interlocking located just west of the station.
(Mike Kopach, ELHS Archives Collection)

RIGHT • Train #28 stops short of Solon Road in Solon to discharge passengers in August 1975. Trains #28 and 29 were operated with pride and punctuality to the end in January 1977. *(Mike Kopach, ELHS Archives Collection)*

LEFT • Train #28, led by E8a #829, gets a "high-ball" from the conductor to depart Geauga Lake in July 1974. The three-car train was well patronized west of Garrettsville-Hiram at this time.
(Mike Kopach, ELHS Archives Collection)

ABOVE • Fireman W. S. "Bill" Duda steps out onto the walkway of GP7 #1401 as train #28 stops at Aurora to discharge passengers in August 1976. Aurora, located 24 miles from Cleveland, is a very affluent bedroom community and a source of substantial passenger ridership for this service. The covered hopper on the team track is a "hold" car to be placed at a later date at Carlon Products, Aurora's only rail served industry located a few miles to the east.
(Mike Kopach, ELHS Archives Collection)

ABOVE • GP35 #2558 and SDP45 #3641 will have no trouble hauling the 110 cars of ore from North Randall to the mills of the Mahoning Valley. Passing through Geauga Lake, OH in this July 1974 photo, it's interesting to note that the train is made up of 70-ton capacity hoppers, the maximum size that could be handled by the ore dumpers at the steel mills. The EL's fairly new "gold stripes" stand out in contrast to the drab foreign cars, including the head car owned by the Clinchfield RR. *(Mike Kopach, ELHS Archives Collection)*

LEAVITTSBURG

Leavittsburg was "the" hotspot for Mahoning Division operations. The main line from Kent to Meadville reduced from double to single track at SN Jct., just west of Leavittsburg. SN Jct. was a 64-lever Saxbe & Farmer interlocking plant that guided trains to and from Cleveland, Kent, Youngstown and Meadville. The location was manned 24/7 as was the Leavittsburg Yard Office. Leavittsburg was an outpost terminal for crews manning the yard and local trains at Leavittsburg and the highly industrialized North Warren area. Four yard crews per day worked out of Leavittsburg as well as a morning local to Kent and an evening local to Ravenna. Leavittsburg was a transfer point for cars coming from Meadville and Kent destined to Cleveland and North Randall. Additionally, an early piggyback ramp installation was located on a stub track near South Leavitt Road. A small engine terminal was home to three Baldwin or Lima switchers and an Alco road unit.

RIGHT, TOP • The Alco 900-series RS2 and RS3 units were bumped from prestige commuter assignments by the arrival of the NJ DOT-funded U34ch units purchased between 1970 and 1973. The vintage Alcos were sent west for their final years to replace Baldwin and Lima switchers on yard and local freights. Well-worn RS2 #910 rests on the engine track at Leavittsburg on July 13, 1973.

(Michael A. Tedesco, ELHS Archives Collection)

RIGHT, CENTER • Another reassigned Alco RS3 is at Leavittsburg in September 1974. A dirty, faded and oil-covered #920 sits on the Piggyback Track with a caboose between assignments. The high-level MU hose connections for units equipped with schedule 6-SL brake equipment can be seen near the end walkway of this unit. *(ELHS Archives Collection)*

RIGHT • U25b #2521 waits on the westbound main track at South Leavitt Road crossing, probably for conflicting traffic at SN Jct., located 0.4 miles west of the crossing. An Alco C425 waits for assignment on the piggyback track. Leavittsburg was a busy location with many trains stopping daily to set off and pick up cars from the industries gathered by the yard and local crews. *(Frank Vollhardt, ELHS Archives Collection)*

ABOVE • Alco C425 #2451, the first of a dozen-unit order for EL, suns itself on the engine track at Leavittsburg on September 7, 1975. The 2500 HP Alco units frequented the Mahoning Division on mainline freights as well as mineral drags and local trains. The units performed well and were destined to go to Conrail. The units were assigned Conrail numbers, but a week before it was to happen the entire class was sold to the British Columbia Railway where #2451 was assigned BCR #801. As fate would have it, the unit has returned to former Erie Lackawanna rails as Delaware-Lackawanna Railway #2451 working out of Scranton, PA. *(David H. Hamley, ELHS Archives Collection)*

ABOVE • The engineer of GP35 #2556 watches for the signal at SN Jct. to make a move back to his train. The engine is located on the 2nd Sub-Division main track east of SN Jct. and has probably just made a set-off in the westbound siding in this April 3, 1976 photo. *(David H. Hamley, ELHS Archives Collection)*

RIGHT • Two weeks prior to Conrail, Alco C424 #2407 waits for the next assignment as it is seen on the Engine Track at Leavittsburg on March 14, 1976. The 13-year-old 2400 HP unit was delivered in a black and yellow paint scheme and looks a bit worn and dirty here but it has served its owner well and will for a few more years before being retired. Amazingly, 35 years later this locomotive survives, working on former Erie Lackawanna trackage carrying the lettering of the Livonia, Avon & Lakeville RR #423, and once again, in black and yellow paint. *(David H. Hamley, ELHS Archives Collection)*

RIGHT • A common sight at Leavittsburg was a trio of Baldwin or Lima switchers used on the SB Yard Jobs that switched the yard and served the industries at North Warren. Baldwin S12 #627 sets on the Engine Track at Leavittsburg in March 1971. By the following year the unit will have been retired. *(Ron Rohrbaugh, ELHS Archives Collection)*

While Leavittsburg was a hotspot, the Youngstown area could quickly become a chokepoint and taxed the wits of the best of operating personnel. The Mahoning Valley was a double track line in which trains moved using Automatic Block Signals. From west to east, there was a connection with the B&O at Warren where hot metal trains from Youngstown accessed the Republic Steel Plant. Further east, near Deforest, was the location of the Pipeline Tracks and eastbound siding where ore from Cleveland and Creston was set off for the B&O to deliver to Republic Steel. The B&O's Lake Branch crossed the EL main tracks at Deforest Tower, a 24/7 manned mechanical interlocking station. Just east of Deforest was Niles where several industries were served by three yard crews per day using rugged Baldwin and Lima switch engines. The Lisbon Branch ran 33.2 miles from Niles to Lisbon where coal was loaded for Ohio Edison's Niles Power Plant as well as for Standard Oil at Cleveland. The Lisbon Branch trains often were powered by a matched A-B-B-A set of F units or RS3s. Continuing east from Niles one came across Mosier Yard; a seven-track yard where empty ore hoppers were stored and inspected prior to moving to the docks. At the east end of Mosier Yard, Girard Siding ran to Brier Hill with a connection to the Canal Branch where the massive US Steel's Ohio Works was accessed. The Joint Yard on the Canal Branch was also used by the PRR and LE&E crews to deliver ore and pull empty hoppers.

Brier Hill was the location of a car shop and large locomotive shop as well as a carpenter, plumbing, signal and Maintenance-of-Way shops. The complex housed the local Trainmaster, Road Foreman of Engines, Master Mechanic, General Car Foreman and support staff. Round-the-clock yard crews worked both ends of the yard and an additional five crews a day worked as captive crews inside the Brier Hill Works of the Youngstown Sheet & Tube Company, which was located just south of the EL tracks. Drag crews operated several times a day between Brier Hill Yard and NK Yard near Center Street on the Haselton Branch and also between Brier Hill and the P&LE Yard at East Youngstown. The normal interchange between EL and P&LE usually ran about 200 cars per day in each direction. This was in addition to ore traffic moving from the EL to P&LE mills in Aliquippa, Neville Island, Pittsburgh and Monessen, PA.

East of Brier Hill at Worthington Street was the junction where the Youngstown & Austintown Branch headed south across the PRR, LE&E and B&O lines to serve the industries on Youngstown's southwest side. A mile further east was the location of the Youngstown Freight House and the North Avenue Coach Yards that supported the passenger operations at the depot. A depot switch crew was on duty each trick of the day to handle the addition and set-off of storage mail, Pullman and Tavern Lounge cars on the Hoboken to Chicago trains and provided the train make-up for the Cleveland trains. In early EL days, two daily trains in each direction operated through from Cleveland to Pittsburgh in a joint EL-P&LE operation. Those trains sometimes consisted of Parlor Lounge cars and other equipment requiring switching at Youngstown.

The Youngstown Passenger Station was located at 112 West Commerce Street in a six-floor building known as the Erie Terminal Building that was later renamed The Binama Building. It was also the home of the Division Offices of the Mahoning Division. The entire place was used by the railroad, save for a flower shop, a doctor's office and a luncheonette on the street level, adjacent to the passenger waiting room and ticket office.

A half-mile east of the depot was an important junction known as Himrod Jct. where the double track Haselton Branch split away from the main and headed to the P&LE at East Youngstown. Between Himrod Jct. and Center Street (P&LE junction) was the location of NK Yard, a major support yard for the steel industry on Youngstown's east side.

Continuing east on the main line from Himrod Jct. was Valley Street where the EL's double track crossed the double track of the New York Central's Youngstown Branch. The electrically-operated interlocking was manned 24/7 by EL operators. East of Valley Street the EL served several industries on the south side of the line, consisting of A&P Foods, Republic Rubber Company, Republic Steel's Truscon Division and several others. The Mahoning Valley was a beehive of activity and dispatching it, especially on second trick, was a tedious job.

BELOW • A former DL&W caboose is seen at Niles Yard on August 11, 1976. When this photo was taken, the Niles & Lisbon Branch was severed with only the end points still having service from Niles and Salem. Conrail retained caboose C-858 at Niles to be used by the abbreviated Niles &Lisbon Branch local.

(Robert Todten, ELHS Archives Collection)

RIGHT • When Conrail was formed, trains #28 and 29 were down to two or three coaches that were handled by a single E8 or GP7. GP7 #1401 arrives at Youngstown with #28 in August 1976, the final summer of operation. Immediately behind the locomotive is the Strouss' Department Store parking garage and to the right, the former Erie Terminal Building, known in 1976 as The Binama Building. Today the train is gone, as are the tracks, the parking deck, and the Phelps Street footbridge. The Binama Building is now a Mahoning County office building.
(ELHS Archives Collection)

ABOVE • The Higbee's Department Store parking garage is in this view of Train #28 arriving at Youngstown. The train would soon pull east to Walnut Street, cross over and then back into the New Siding along the wall for the night and the GP7 would run lite to Brier Hill for servicing.
(ELHS Archives Collection)

RIGHT • In a view taken from one of the coaches on Train #28, the photographer captured a ritual performed several times a day, 365 days a year: a hot metal train returning to Republic Steel's Haselton Furnace in Youngstown from the Warren Plant. The train is setting on the B&O's Old Line and as soon as #28 departs Warren, the crew will obtain permission to shove out onto the eastbound and follow #28 to Youngstown.
(Mike Kopach, ELHS Archives Collection)

ABOVE • What commuter wouldn't like these accommodations? This is the interior of one of the former DL&W lightweight coaches used on Train #28 and #29 in the mid-1970s.

(Mike Kopach, ELHS Archives Collection)

BELOW • Former Lackawanna lightweight coach #306, now bearing EL #1306 and along with two sisters, is on weekend layover in the New Siding at Youngstown. The train is on standby steam in this March 1976 photo. *(ELHS Archives Collection)*

ABOVE • A pair of high-horsepower GE six-axle units, led by U33c #3307 drifts downgrade at Hazel Street near the Youngstown Passenger Station in this March 1976 photo. The stacks in the background are those of Ohio Edison's North Avenue Steam Plant that provides steam heat to downtown buildings, including the Binama Building where the Mahoning Division offices are located.

(Mike Kopach, ELHS Archives Collection)

LEFT • The crossing watchman's shanty at Hazel Street in Youngstown did not afford many amenities, so on this August day in 1975 the watchman reposes on a lawn chair and chats with a pedestrian. Hazel Street was one-way, uphill and during the heavier passenger days, it was quite a busy location with cars being added and removed from the trains as well as switching to the Terminal Track and the coach yard.

(ELHS Archives Collection)

ABOVE • Brier Hill was the home to EL 03301, one of EL's 250-ton capacity Industrial Brownhoist derricks. The crane was built in 1954 at an undisclosed cost and tipped the scales at 385,000 lbs. The diesel-powered unit was conveyed to Conrail as #50211. A smaller, 160-ton capacity crane was previously assigned to Youngstown but the larger crane was required for derailments of Hot Metal cars. The crane, idler and additional support cars are seen on the Wrecker Track at Brier Hill on May 10, 1975. The entire wreck train consist numbered about six cars, which included a kitchen-dining car and a sleeper-office car. *(Ron Rohrbaugh, ELHS Archives Collection)*

ABOVE • Alco RS3 #1057 switches at the East End of Brier Hill Yard at Youngstown in March 1975. The unit was a combination of the frame of former Erie/EL RS3 #929 and the carbody from former Boston & Maine #1507. The surgery was performed at Hornell Shop in September 1973. If you look closely behind the nearest marker light you can see the remaining steam generator stack from the B&M days. The unit was retired in October 1976. *(Mike Kopach, ELHS Archives Collection)*

ABOVE • Brier Hill Diesel Shop, known as "DO" Shop, was always a hotbed of motive power and an inviting location for photographers. It had an easy in/out from the main road, locomotives were close to the parking lot and the officials were friendly to responsible railfans.

Mike shot this view in the EL's last days of March 1976. The ready and service tracks are ripe with Alco RS2, RS3 and C424s in addition to EMD SD45s and a couple of GP7s. A spare passenger coach for the Cleveland train is near the Speed Repair Track.

(Mike Kopach, ELHS Archives Collection)

ABOVE • Another view of the motive power at Brier Hill in March 1976 shows the sand towers and fueling stations. *(Mike Kopach, ELHS Archives Collection)*

ABOVE • Train 178 has arrived at VO Crossover and is pulling the setoff into the South Yard Extension at Brier Hill in March 1976 behind F7a #6351, F7a #6331 and F7b #6352. Soon the train will make a pickup of cars for Meadville and east. Brier Hill produced two considerable pickups per day in each direction for Train #94 and #178 eastbound and Train #95 and #187 westbound. The fence behind the train protects the property of the Youngstown Sheet & Tube Company's Brier Hill Works. *(Mike Kopach, ELHS Archives Collection)*

ABOVE • In this second view the train has pulled toward #2 South Yard and cut the rear of the train off at VO Crossover. At this time, the power and setoff will pull to the East End of Brier Hill, leave the setoff in the South Yard and cross over to the main yard and make a pickup, pull out to the eastward main and then shove the pickup back toward VO and depart for Ferrona and Meadville. Rituals such as this were performed a few times a day at Brier Hill, a flat switching yard that was quite efficient.

(Mike Kopach, ELHS Archives Collection)

ABOVE • A cut of local service caboose cars and M-of-W service tool cars are spotted in the South Yard at the East End of Brier Hill in this March 1976 photo.

The footbridge over the tracks belongs to the Youngstown Sheet & Tube Company for their employees to access the Brier Hill Works. *(Mike Kopach, ELHS Archives Collection)*

ABOVE • In 1969 the EL built several Transfer Caboose cars at the Meadville Program Car Shop for yard and transfer runs. In this February 1977 photo we see former Youngstown car #T-22 at an unknown location. The waycars were fitted with a desk and two benches, a heat-ing stove and a dry sink with a small portable water tank mounted above. The transfer cabooses were not a favorite of the crews and were used basically for short runs such as interchange drags and Hot Metal Trains. *(Mike Kopach, ELHS Archives Collection)*

ABOVE • A five-unit consist of second-generation power representing all three major builders backs toward the diesel shop from the East End of Brier Hill.

Most likely, the three GE units will be removed at the shop for ore service and the train will continue east with #2453 and #2565. The view is from the YS&T footbridge.

(William F. Herrmann, ELHS Archives Collection)

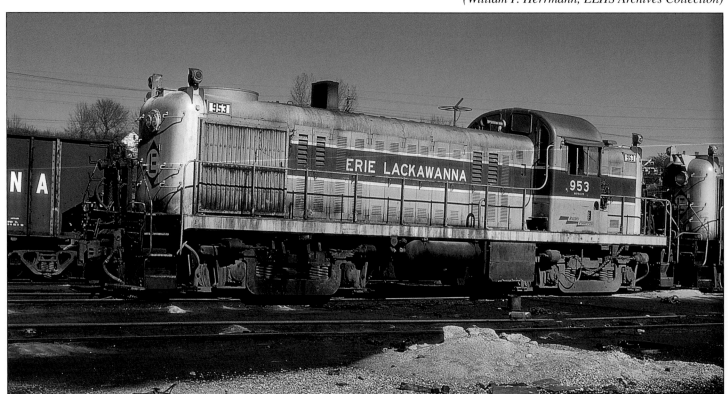

ABOVE • Originally assigned #1003 when built in December 1949, Alco RS2 was renumbered to #953 when a steam generator was added at Hornell Shop in 1954. Excess steam generators were available from F3s that had been replaced with the E8s and additional diesel power was needed for commuter service.

After the U34ch units were delivered, the 900 series Alcos landed in Meadville, Youngstown and Marion for yard and local service. The unit was photographed at Brier Hill on March 10, 1974.

(David H. Hamley, ELHS Archives Collection)

ABOVE • A dozen former Lackawanna Fairbanks-Morse H24-66 Train Masters wandered westward after the EL merger and were assigned to Brier Hill Shop. The units were terrific for ore service since three units could handle 110 loads of ore easily between Cleveland and Youngstown or Sharon. Additionally, single units were ideal for transfer drags, Shenango Turns and main line locals in the Youngstown area. Class MFFM-24D-6 #1861 is at the West End of Brier Hill in August 1970 tacking caboose C-209 onto a drag for NK Yard. Soon the beast will run to the east end and tie on and depart for NK Yard using the 2400 HP to start the train and the powerful dynamic brakes to control the movement downgrade to destination. A Baldwin switcher sits on the Extension Track and another goes about its business with a captive crew in the Brier Hill Works, which was originally known as The Brier Hill Steel Co. *(Stephen M. Timko)*

ABOVE • Derrick #03131, a 160-ton capacity Bucyrus-Erie product, was built in 1927 as a steam derrick and the Erie Railroad converted it to diesel at Hornell Shop in December 1958. The 268,400-lb. unit was equipped with a Kim Hot Start to keep the cooling water from freezing in cold weather. After several incidents involving derailed hot metal bottles, the Brier Hill derrick was exchanged for the larger 250-ton capacity unit #03301. The entire wrecking outfit was kept ready for action on the Wrecker Track at the Brier Hill Diesel Shop where it is seen in this August 1970 photo. *(Stephen M. Timko)*

LEFT • A major flurry of activity is taking place at the East End of Brier Hill Yard in this photo taken from the YS&T employee footbridge in 1972. An eastbound train is backing a setoff into the New Yard at the far left and will double to the caboose on the eastbound main beyond the Division Street Bridge. Another set of power, EMD F units, is arriving from Cleveland on train 156, having crossed into the yard at VO or the West End of Brier Hill. Two Baldwin switchers are seen: one working the lead and the other waiting to cross a cut of coke to the Youngstown Sheet & Tube's Brier Hill Works to the far right. Some track relocations have taken place to allow construction of Route 711 and a new bridge next to the Division Street Bridge. Construction materials can be seen to the far left behind the East End Yard Office, which by the way, sports a new roof. The YS&T sintering plant and closed coke works as well as the ore yard and ore bridge can be seen to the right. YS&T's Brier Hill Works coke plant was constructed in 1918 and was completely rebuilt in 1960, but it was never operated after the rebuild. The plant contained 84 Koppers ovens.
(William F. Herrmann, ELHS Archives Collection)

ABOVE • A pair of EMD NW2s is alongside the Brier Hill Shop Offices in December 1978. Alco RS3 #1049 waits for attention at the shop. The 1049 is a former Lackawanna unit and was equipped with 24RL brake equipment and could MU with other road power.

The former Erie RS3 units were equipped with 6SL brake equipment and would not MU with most other road power.

(Mike Kopach, ELHS Archives Collection)

ABOVE • We're into Conrail in this August 11, 1976 photo of EL RS3 #1020 at Brier Hill Shop, but the renumbering has not taken place as of yet. The 1600 HP unit, showing its deck-level MU connections for the 6SL brake schedule, will eventually wear Conrail #5240.

Brier Hill Shop gained some additional work by doing maintenance and inspections on former PC units assigned to the Youngstown area that previously were handled at Conway. *(ELHS Archives Collection)*

ABOVE • A well-lighted Alco RS2 #913 is at Brier Hill on January 25, 1973. The short hood contains a steam generator for passenger service. While the units were removed from commuter varnish in the early 1970s, several retained their steam generators and actually were used as pinch hitters on trains #28 and 29 when needed.

(Ron Rohrbaugh, ELHS Archives Collection)

BELOW • F3a #6621 is MU'ed to RS3 #1045 at NK Yard on the Haselton Branch at Youngstown on October 2, 1972. This is unusual power to be at NK Yard, but it could be pinch-hitting on a Brier Hill — NK Drag or a transfer run to the P&LE at East Youngstown.

(Ron Rohrbaugh, ELHS Archives Collection)

ABOVE • A close-up view of transfer caboose T-24at is seen at Scranton, PA in August 1971. While not on the Mahoning Division, the car was assigned here and the nice ¾ view may help the modelers. *(Ron Rohrbaugh, ELHS Archives Collection)*

ABOVE • The steel industry of the Mahoning and Shenango Valley required an ample supply of gondolas for outbound shipments. Iron and steel products were shipped in gondolas, boxcars and flatcars. The EL 43000 series bulkhead gons were assigned to Youngstown for pipe loading out of Republic Steel and Youngstown Sheet & Tube Co. The 65-foot, 70-ton capacity car is stenciled "When empty return to EL RY Youngstown, OH." The car retains those markings in this October 1988 photo. *(Mike Kopach, ELHS Archives Collection)*

ABOVE • EL 15677 is a 65-foot, low side, wood floor gondola assigned to steel loading.

The 75-ton capacity gondola measured 65 feet, 6 inches inside and 70' 8" outside and was built by on-line industry Greenville Steel Car Company of Greenville, PA. *(Mike Kopach, ELHS Archives Collection)*

ORE SHIPMENTS ORIGINATING OFF-LINE AND MOVING VIA MAHONING DIVISION - 1975:

DOCK	CONSIGNEE	ROUTE	CARS	TONS
Conneaut-B&LE	Sharon Steel Company-Farrell	B&LE-Shenango-EL	3,782	252,011
Conneaut-B&LE	Republic Steel Corporation-Warren	B&LE-Shenango-EL (B&O Dely)	3,252	261,743
Conneaut-B&LE	Republic Steel Corporation—Youngstown	B&LE-Shenango-EL	3,453	263,110
Conneaut-B&LE	Youngstown Sheet & Tube Corp-Campbell Works	B&LE-Shenango-EL (P&LE Dely)	834	59,843
Conneaut-B&LE	Youngstown Sheet & Tube Corp-Brier Hill Works	B&LE-Shenango-EL	883	67,008
Conneaut-B&LE	US Steel Corp-Ohio Works	B&LE-Shenango-EL	633	47,281
Conneaut-B&LE	Republic Steel Corp-Buffalo NY	B&LE-Shenango-EL	250	18,126
River Terminal RR	Republic Steel Corporation-Warren	RT-N&SS-Aetna Rd-EL (B&O Dely)	1,753	125,727
River Terminal RR	Republic Steel Corporation-Youngstown	RT-N&SS-Aetna Rd-EL	1,002	72,005
Huron (N&W)	Republic Steel Corporation-Warren	N&W-Creston-EL (B&O Dely)	1,535	125,323
Huron (N&W)	Republic Steel Corporation-Youngstown	N&W-Creston-EL	254	22,582
Huron (N&W)	Youngstown Sheet & Tube Corp.-Campbell Works	N&W-Creston-EL (P&LE Dely)	4,331	297,036
Huron (N&W)	Youngstown Sheet & Tube Corp-Brier Hill Works	N&W-Creston-EL	1,510	103,302
TOTAL			**23,472**	**1,715,097**

ABOVE • We're a few months into Conrail but you can't tell it from this photo. Former DL&W Alco RS3 #1051 is seen in the company of a sister unit on the service tracks at Brier Hill Shop on September 19, 1976. Consists of two, three, or four RS3s were common on Shenango Turns, Cleveland Extras and other division freight trains. *(David H. Hamley, ELHS Archives Collection)*

ABOVE • GP35 #2554 is seen at the west end of the Brier Hill Diesel Shop on May 21, 1977. A strange bedfellow is present in the form of Detroit Edison U30c #010 and an additional unidentified unit. The DE units were used on unit coal trains between the former Monongahela RR and the Detroit Edison power plant in Monroe, MI.

Five units were used on a train of 140 cars, three units on the head-end, and two operated by radio-remote-control two-thirds of the way back in the train. They didn't operate over EL but the power came to Brier Hill for attention as seen in this photo.

(David H. Hamley, ELHS Archives Collection)

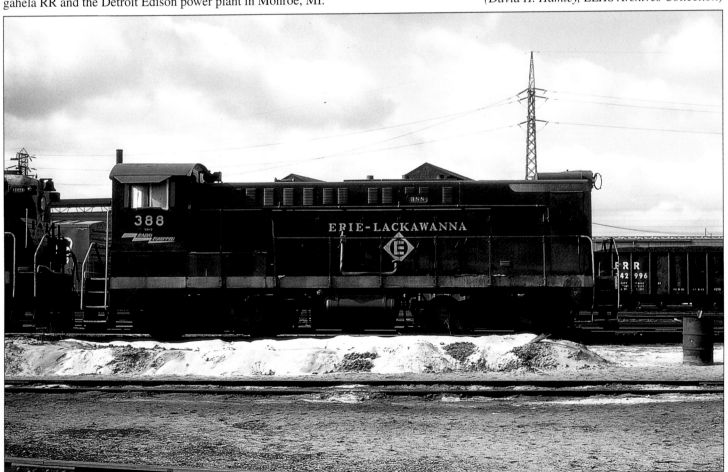

ABOVE • During the 1960s, Brier Hill was Baldwin territory, both for yard and local service. Former Erie Baldwin DS44-750, class SB-7 is out of service on February 27, 1969.

Sharing the track is AS16 #1109. The Baldwin era was rapidly coming to an end on EL at this time. *(ELHS Archives Collection)*

ABOVE • Railroads and the steel industry worked hand-in-hand in the Mahoning Valley. In this March 1976 photo we see Youngstown Sheet & Tube Company Alco S1 switcher #664 at the West End of Brier Hill working alongside EL RS3 #1028. In addition to delivering and pulling freight to and from the steel producer, EL also operated five crews per day inside the YS&T's Brier Hill Works as captive crews. These crews performed under the direction of the YS&T Yardmaster and were paid for entirely by Sheet & Tube.

(Mike Kopach, ELHS Archives Collection)

ABOVE • Conrail is only a month away as RS3 #1009 and caboose C-137 make a move on the Wall Track at Center Street in Youngstown. Republic Steel's Haselton Furnace forms the backdrop in this photo. All is well with the economy in Youngstown at this time but the massive Republic operation only lasted about six more years. *(ELHS Archives Collection)*

ABOVE • The photographer slipped into the YS&T Brier Hill Works to capture this shot of RS3 #1013 in March 1976. Many of us have tried similar stunts at this location in the name of getting a rare photograph, but it was usually to take a picture of one of the bright orange YS&T Alcos or Baldwins. The unit is assigned to the captive crews that work inside the "Brier Hill Steel."

(Dennis M. Kupetz, ELHS Archives Collection)

BELOW • It's the summer of 1976 but there's no sign of Conrail in this photo. Alco C424 #2409 throttles up as it passes the former location of NK Target on its way to Brier Hill. The former NYC passenger station is out of view to the right and the hand-operated target in the photo allows the B&O to access the former PC interchange. The buildings to the right are the downtown Youngstown skyline.

(ELHS Archives Collection)

The Shenango Valley was a highly industrialized area near Sharon, PA that grew along the banks of the Shenango River. The area between Hubbard, OH and Sharpsville, PA was served out of the former Erie's Ferrona Yard on Sharon's northeast side. The yard was home to a half-dozen Baldwin or Lima yard engines and an Alco RS3 for the New Castle Local. The New Castle Branch ran south 23 miles along the river to New Castle where it interchanged with the B&O, P&LE and PRR. The P&LE had trackage rights over the EL's New Castle Branch and operated a nightly train over that route. The long and impressive list of industries in the Shenango Valley in-

cluded: Sharon Steel, National Malleable Castings, Wheatland Tube, Sharon Tube, J. B. Goldberg Scrap Company, Sawhill Tube, General American Tank Car (GATX), Petroleum Iron Works, The Ivor J. Lee Company, Golden Dawn Food Stores, Shenango Incorporated, and many others. To add to the congestion in the area, the main line possessed three sections of single track between Hubbard and Pymatuning. The NYC crossed the EL at State Line Interlocking to access Sharon Steel and also accessed Ferrona Yard through hand-operated main track switches at Ferrona.

ABOVE • Alco RS3 #918 switches at Ferrona Yard, Sharon, PA as the crossing watchman protects Clark Street for the movement. The Sawhill Tube Company, an Erie Lackawanna customer, forms the background in this June 1974 photo. *(Mike Kopach, ELHS Archives Collection)*

LEFT • Stenciling indicates that caboose C128 was painted at Meadville 11-73. The colorful caboose is seen during switching moves at Ferrona Yard in June 1974. *(Mike Kopach, ELHS Archives Collection)*

LEFT • Alco RS3 #1026 shuffles some empty coke hoppers on the "high side" at the east end of Ferrona Yard on May 22, 1976. The N&W hoppers arrived at Ferrona loaded with coke from the Jewell Smokeless Coal and Coke Company of Vansant, VA via N&W-Marion-EL. Sharon Steel's coke plant was dismantled a half-century prior to this photo. *(David H. Hamley, ELHS Archives Collection)*

The main line from Kent to Meadville is an 89-mile saw tooth line that was a challenge to locomotive engineers operating in either direction but was especially troublesome for eastbound trains. While we consider Kent the western terminus of the Mahoning Division, the division point was actually a few miles further east at Brady Lake, MP 188.4. The operating crews from Meadville and Youngstown operated as far west as Crane Avenue Kent with the passenger crews operating nearly another mile to the Kent Depot.

The main line, known as the 2nd Sub-Division, was double track from Kent to SN Jct. where the track became single track to Pymatuning, PA, governed by CTC controlled by the operator at SN Jct. From Pymatuning to Shenango it was again double track. From Shenango to BK Tower located at the west end of Meadville Yard the line was again CTC under the control of the operator at BK Jct. The NYC crossed the 2nd Sub-Division at Braceville, Latimer and Amasa, the B&O crossed at North Warren as did the PRR who also crossed at Bruin while the B&LE crossed at Shenango. The B&LE also had a hand-thrown connection at French Creek just west of BK.

ABOVE • A westbound train is parked on Kent West Yard #1 track in February 1971. Behind the U25b and the six-axle GE are cars that were picked up at Shenango, PA.

Noted in the train is a new Bucyrus-Erie crawler crane built in Erie, PA that routed B&LE-Shenango-EL and a block of new 100-foot high-cube L&N boxcars built at Greenville Steel Car Company at Greenville, PA. *(ELHS Archives Collection)*

ABOVE • On October 2, 1971 Track #1 Kent West Yard contains a Creston Turn consisting of mainly empty ore hoppers being returned to the N&W to be reloaded at the Huron Dock. The Alco C425 and the EMD SD45 will likely return to Kent in about six hours with another train of ore for the blast furnaces of the Mahoning Valley. In track #2 another SD45 leads a mixed train, probably #95 or #187 for switching at Marion.

The manifest trains such as train #74, 98, 99, 100 etc. ran through Kent without stopping for crew changes but the secondary trains that worked along the division still changed crews at Kent. The college town provided ample food, lodging and entertainment options for the crew members between assignments. EL train crews shared rooms at the Kent Motor Inn, as did the engine crews, resulting in the use of nearly 40 hotel rooms per day. *(ELHS Archives Collection)*

ABOVE • F3a #6311, a 1948 EMD product, leads an unidentified U25b as it waits on Kent West Yard #1 track in June 1971 for a rested crew to run to Marion.

The train could quite possibly be #95, a train generally consisting of empty cars returning to the west. The west end of #1 and #2 East Yard can be seen in this photo. *(ELHS Archives Collection)*

ABOVE • GE U25b #2511 is in the lead on Track #1 Kent West Yard on a gray Ohio day in September 1972. The train provides an interesting view with an odd mix of motive power. The U-boat leads an Alco C424, an Alco RS3, two EMD F7bs and a GP35. The train, probably #95, is a westbound Meadville make-up train that is transporting due or dead power to Marion Shop.

The train has picked up a High & Wide shipment at Shenango out of Cooper-Bessemer at Grove City and then picked up at Pymatuning Siding a couple of transformers out of Westinghouse at Sharon, PA that could only move via the Second Subdivision due to 18'6" bridge clearance through Youngstown.

(Mike Kopach, ELHS Archives Collection)

ABOVE • Hidden in the previous photo, another westbound train waits for a crew in #2 Kent West Yard in September 1972.

The nine-year old Alco C424's were rough riders but performed well for the EL. *(Mike Kopach, ELHS Archives Collection)*

A westbound departs Kent with SD45 #3612 leading #3315, the highest numbered EL U33c, as it approaches the Main Street crossing in December 1974. The B&O main tracks are below along the Cuyahoga River and behind the train is the Williams Brothers Milling Company, a long-time EL and Erie customer in downtown Kent.
(Mike Kopach, ELHS Archives Collection)

ABOVE • The details are cloudy, but it appears that a westbound train on the main track has sideswiped a train departing #1 Kent West Yard in the spring of 1976. Perhaps it was one of those classic Conrail Day One incidents that we all had to face. At any rate, train wrecks bring out the spectators, as seen in this photo at Crane Avenue. Hulcher is preparing to make a lift on U36c #3324. It's a good thing the excessive dimension transformer in the photo wasn't involved in the accident! *(Mike Kopach, ELHS Archives Collection)*

ABOVE • Hulcher's forces move some ties into place to stabilize the sidewinder prior to making a lift on the big GE. Wrecking is a long, tiring, and dangerous job. *(Mike Kopach, ELHS Archives Collection)*

LEFT • With a sidewinder on each side of the rear end, Hulcher prepares to rerail the #3324, probably toward the eastbound main track. It would take four of the big Cats to completely "lift and walk" the big GE to stable track. While the derailment was clearly on the former Kent Division, Mahoning Division Superintendent W. E. "Bill" Flight, in the brown overcoat, accesses the damage.
(Mike Kopach, ELHS Archives Collection)

BELOW • With the big GE out of the way, Hulcher is setting an SD45 back on firm footing.
(Mike Kopach, ELHS Archives Collection)

RIGHT • North Warren on the Second Sub-Division was a highly industrialized area with dozens of rail loading docks and rail doors. The area produced light bulbs, automobile wiring harnesses, pipe, coil steel, welding machines, railroad car forgings, induction heating furnaces, and many other products. The territory was worked by three daily yard crews, one on each shift out of Leavittsburg Yard. Standard motive power was a 1000 or 1200 HP Lima or Baldwin switch engine. EL #615, a Baldwin DS44-1000, shoves an empty box car out of Packard Plant #10 down the Back Track at North Warren in April 1970. The GN car originally contained copper billets used to make automobile wiring at Packard Electric Company. The PRR's WN Tower is in the view to the right. WN controlled the EL crossing of the PY&A Division of the PRR. *(ELHS Archives Collection)*

BELOW • Two of Erie Lackawanna's premier piggyback trains meet at Johnsons, OH in March 1976. NY99 holds the main track as the NY98 pulls through the 165-car-length siding. When the caboose clears, the operator at SN Jct. will line the switch and signal and the NY99 will roll westward through Cortland, North Warren, Leavittsburg, and points west. The crews on these trains are inter-divisional crews, meaning they operate between Meadville and Marion with employees from either terminal manning either train. The IDR crew agreement enhanced time sensitive schedules by eliminating crew changes at Kent, OH and Salamanca, NY. Soon all of that will change with the coming of Conrail on April 1st. *(Ron Rohrbaugh, ELHS Archives Collection)*

LEFT • XN Tower, Shenango, PA controlled the crossing of the Erie Lackawanna's Main Line with the Bessemer & Lake Erie's Low Grade Line just west of Greenville, PA. The tower, originally manned 50% by employees of each road, was fully staffed by EL personnel when this photo was taken on July 27, 1983. The tower, under Conrail ownership, has received a new coat of paint and a new roof. Train orders were nearly a thing of the past by this date, but the "iron man" is still in place to allow high-speed delivery of train orders to eastbound EL trains. The EL reduced from double to single track eastbound at XN and the B&LE did likewise southbound. The restroom was located in the basement with the oil furnace and the interlocking mechanism. The structure and the mechanical-operated switches were retired by Conrail. Single track remains with an automatic interlocking. *(ELHS Archives Collection)*

ERIE LACKAWANNA – BESSEMER & LAKE ERIE RR SHENANGO INTERCHANGE FIGURES

YEAR	EL TO B&LE (REVENUE CARS)	B&LE TO EL (REVENUE CARS)
1968	2,958	6,911
1969	2,515	17,091

RIGHT • A pair of 45's, SDP45 #3654 and SD45 #3623, powers a westbound train through Shenango, PA in June 1974. The roof of XN Tower is above the train. The four-track yard in the foreground is the New Yard while the four-track Old Yard is out of view to the left. *(Mike Kopach, ELHS Archives Collection)*

RIGHT, BOTTOM • The passing siding at Amasa, PA, located between Greenville and Atlantic, was the shortest controlled siding between Kent and Meadville with a capacity of 118 cars. Equipped with a spring switch on the east end, it was basically used for clearing short eastbound trains in order to meet a westbound train. A westbound mixed freight train passes through the automatic interlocking where the former NYC's Stoneboro Branch crosses the EL at the east end of Amasa in June 1974 behind SD45 #3604 and E8a #821. The Bessemer & Lake Erie's high line passes overhead, while the low line crossed the EL at grade at Shenango, 4.9 miles west of Amasa. A section of the overhead bridge was destroyed by an EL derailment about ten years prior to this photo.
(Mike Kopach, ELHS Archives Collection)

BK Jct. or "Buchanan," was the junction of the Oil City Branch that ran 34 miles to Franklin and Oil City. BK was also the east end of the single track from Shenango. Meadville Yards begin just east of BK with the Westbound Yard and the Eastbound Yard on their respective sides. Meadville also was the location of a small diesel shop that serviced the yard engines assigned to Meadville, Oil City, Jamestown and Salamanca and performed minor repairs to road units needing attention. The shop was small – it housed only two units and did inspections and light repairs, yet the lo-

cation was a constant maze; it cut power apart and made up locomotive consists for outbound trains and funneled locomotives to Hornell and Marion for heavy maintenance. Meadville also housed a System Program Car Shop, a Reclamation Plant, a Cripple Track (for running car repairs), a Motor Car Shop, a Hi-Rail Shop, an Oil Test Lab, an Air Brake Shop, a Carpenter Shop, a Plumbers Shop and a Sign Shop. Meadville was also the location of a Trainmaster and a Road Foreman of Engines as well as support staff and crew callers.

LEFT • EL 7418 was a dual-purpose machine that performed as a weed burner in the summer and a snow melter in the winter. The freshly painted machine seen in the M-of-W track off of the Back Lead in Meadville on January 7, 1973 was an important item for keeping the yard fluid. The chain driven machine's four flame throwers were fueled with kerosene or snow burning oil that heated the switch points and rods and greatly reduced the time and work of removing snow by hand.
(Ron Rohrbaugh, ELHS Archives Collection)

ABOVE • Strange-looking Alco S2 #521 moves east on the westbound pull-in track at Meadville in 1972. The unit is part of class MSA-10; the "M" indicating <u>M</u>ultiple unit controls. It was operated with a sister on the light rails of the Oil City Branch.

The odd cab was constructed at Hornell Shop from a retired Baldwin AS16 unit after 521's cab was destroyed in a collision with Train #5 at Kent, OH on December 28, 1962.
(William F. Herrmann, ELHS Archive Collection)

ABOVE • A pair of 45's, SDP45 #3650 and SD45 #3614, works eastbound toward Meadville in this June 1974 photo.

Shortly, the crew will turn this section of train 98 over to a fresh crew for a dash across the former Meadville and Allegany Divisions to Hornell, NY. *(Mike Kopach, ELHS Archives Collection)*

ABOVE • Alco RS3 #923 works the westbound lead at Meadville West Yard in 1969. A half-dozen former New York Division passenger units, including #923, landed at Meadville for service on yard and local trains. The foundation in the foreground is the remains of the old Westbound Yard Office, now relocated to the new tower across the tracks. *(William F. Herrmann, ELHS Archives Collection)*

LEFT • Bumped to freight service after the discontinuance of Trains #5 and 6, fireman Larry Ervin handles the throttle on 7200 HP as it departs westbound from Meadville Yard in 1972. Engineer Paul Mushrush will take over the train-handling duties at Johnsons and the ritual will be repeated at Kent and Ashland on the 202-mile interdivisional trip to Marion, OH. *(William F. Herrmann, ELHS Archives Collection)*

ABOVE • Meadville Diesel Shop was always a beehive of activity whether it was the monthly inspections on the Alco switchers (seen in the shop), fueling mainline hotshots, or cutting and making up consists for outbound trains. What may look unusual to the railfan but was normal to EL employees was this pairing of FM H24-66 Train Master #1854 with F3a #6054. Both are former DL&W units and the FM was originally equipped with a steam generator for passenger service. The power will handle the daily HF98 from Meadville to Salamanca and, after a crew change at that Cattaraugus County location, proceed to Hornell. *(ELHS Archives Collection)*

ABOVE • The late afternoon sun accentuates the as-delivered paint scheme of U25b #2510 at Meadville on August 7, 1974. The ground, saturated with crater lube, fuel oil and lube oil, certainly would not be tolerated in today's environment.

(ELHS Archives Collection)

ABOVE • In Chapter 11 you'll see a camp car assigned to a locomotive crane operator while working at outlying points. Here we see one of the actual cranes: #2910 and idler car EL 434062 at Meadville in September 1977. The Industrial Brownhoist cranes were used to load and unload track material at various locations on the railroad.

(Ron Rorbaugh, ELHS Archive Collection)

BELOW • This is a rear-end view of Brownhoist crane 2910, which were known as "locomotive cranes" due to their self-propelled capability and the fact that they could handle a handful of cars, with air, on the main track with only one trainman. They were frequently seen with a caboose for the trainman's accommodations. The photo was taken in the former Reclamation Shop area of Meadville in October 1978. *(Mike Kopach, ELHS Archives Collection)*

ABOVE • With no varnish to pull, the E8s were assigned to freight service with some being re-geared for lower speed operation. EL #819 is seen at sunrise, looking quite well, on April 14, 1973. The photo was taken at the west end of the Meadville Diesel Shop. The shop had a run-through track (the track where #819 is parked) and could house two switchers. The track in the foreground, nearly out of sight in the sand and oil, was a stub track in the building and would hold one switcher unit. *(David H. Hamley, ELHS Archives Collection)*

ABOVE • When the 900 series Alco road switchers moved west from the commuter zone they replaced many smaller yard locomotives such as the Alco S2 and S4 units at Akron and Marion. That allowed the EMD switchers such as NW2 #412 to find a new home and the EMD "pups" started to arrive at Brier Hill and Meadville, which were previously Baldwin, Lima and Alco strongholds. Well worn, 1948 vintage NW2 #412 is at Meadville Diesel Shop on July 26, 1975.

(David H. Hamley, ELHS Archive Collection)

LEFT • Prior to the influx of the 900-series units at Meadville, the yard was switched by Alco S2 and S4 locomotives, some fitted with MU control and used on the Oil City Branch. Alco S4 #527 is seen MU'ed to two unidentified sisters at Meadville on May 29, 1971. The unit was sold to the Buffalo Creek RR as #52 on November 18, 1973. The Buffalo Creek RR was jointly owned by the EL and the Lehigh Valley RR. *(Charles Housar, ELHS Archives Collection)*

ABOVE • Meadville was a wonderful location to photograph trains in the late afternoon and early evening hours with the railroad on a northeast to southwest heading.

Former Lackawanna F3a #6591 is mated with former Erie F7b #7123 in this 1970 photo. Both locomotives were equipped with dynamic brakes. *(William F. Herrmann, ELHS Archives Collection)*

ABOVE • A trio of Alcos; RS3 #1041 and C424 #2410 are repositioned by the hostler and a laborer at Meadville Diesel Shop as one of the 1000 HP Alco switchers waits under the Smock Bridge. *(William F. Herrmann, ELHS Archives Collection)*

ABOVE • The photographer is onboard a locomotive on the westbound main track at Meadville in this 1973 photo. To the far left is the Back Lead Track and the M-of-W Yard. The coal tipple spanning both main tracks, a reminder of the steam era, stood well into Conrail years.

The Meadville Diesel Shop is to the right of the string of second-generation locomotives. A handful of switchers and a locomotive crane sit on the storage tracks.

(William F. Herrmann, ELHS Archives Collection)

ABOVE • A westbound train pulling into Meadville West Yard provides the background for this set of locomotives on the Eastbound Siding ready to back onto a section of Train #98 for the trip to Hor-

nell, NY in this October 1972 photo. The 9100 HP will be put to task on the many grades in the 186-mile run. *(ELHS Archives Collection)*

ABOVE • EL #1303 Jordan Spreader is an interesting piece of machinery that was rarely used. Jordan Spreaders were expensive to maintain and operate and were very slow to respond and handle. Built to clean ditches, slope hillsides and to grade track shoulders, #1303 was mainly assigned to Meadville for snow fighting duties.

The blades, wings and flanger bars were movable and operated by compressed air from an onboard air compressor and/or air supplied by the main reservoir of the locomotive.

(David H. Hamley, ELHS Archives Collection)

ABOVE • A westbound train designated as Hopper 1X, powered by a lone SDP45 #3653, hauls a train of empty hoppers from Buffalo into Meadville where the crews will change and the train will depart for Marion, OH. The winter snow is nearly a thing of the past in this April 1975 photo. *(ELHS Archives Collection)*

Meadville to Salamanca was formerly part of the Allegany-Meadville Division, which was headquartered in Salamanca, NY. In the fall of 1962, the Allegany-Meadville Division was merged into the Mahoning Division with Meadville to Salamanca becoming the 3rd Sub-Division and the former Allegany Division becoming the 4th Sub-Division.

Meadville to Corry, a distance of 42 miles, is basically a steady slight upgrade line eastbound. Near Millers the eastbound track crosses over the westbound on a bridge and runs "left handed" for about four miles before crossing back over the westbound on another bridge. The EL provided a daily local freight from Meadville to Jamestown, NY to serve local industries at Saegertown, Cambridge Springs, Mill Village, Union City, Corry, Columbus and Lottsville, PA as well as Ashville and Lakewood, NY before turning back from Jamestown. The PRR connected with the EL at Union City and Corry and also crossed the EL at EYE Tower and MS Towers at Corry. East of Corry, the double track became two single track lines between Columbus, PA (CM Jct.) and Niobe, NY (NE Jct.). One line was known as the Columbus & Erie RR (C&E RR) and ran through Lottsville, PA. The other line, known as the Old Line, ran through Bear Lake, PA. The C&E was 4.2 miles longer (13.2 miles between CM and NE). For the most part, in the name of eliminating speed restrictions at each end, the preferred method of operation was eastbound via the C&E and westbound via the Old Line.

East of Niobe, NY the line was double track through Watts Flats, Ashville, Lakewood, and Jamestown to Falconer, NY.

Jamestown at one time had a very large freight house operation as well as a huge industrial base. Reports indicate that during WWII there were nearly a dozen daily yard crews a day working in Jamestown. By the mid-1960's the operation was down to a daylight and an afternoon yard crew and a local that operated to South Dayton on the B&SW Branch.

At DV Tower, Falconer, NY, the NYC's Dunkirk, Allegheny Valley & Pittsburgh Line crossed the double tracked EL line that continued to Waterboro. Waterboro, located at MP 23.0, was the beginning of a single track climb eastbound up Randolph Hill to RH Tower at MP 14. At RH Tower, the line again became a double track line through Steamburg, NY onto the Seneca Indian Reservation to Salamanca where the Dunkirk Branch joined the main line at WC Jct., which was located at the west end of Salamanca Yard.

The Buffalo & Southwestern Branch in the Erie Lackawanna era ran 58.6 miles from Waterboro to BC Jct. near Buffalo. The line runs through Blasdell, Hamburg, Eden Center, Gowanda, Dayton, South Dayton, Cherry Creek, and Conewango Valley before reaching the main line connection at Waterboro, NY. Hampered by a 3%-plus grade ascending westbound between Gowanda and Dayton, the line was nonetheless a haven for local businesses using rail service. In addition to the usual local lumber yards and feed mills the line was home to a very large Carnation Milk Plant at South Dayton, NY, as well as the Peter Cooper Glue Factory at Gowanda, NY.

ABOVE • An interesting angle sees Alco C425 #2457 leaning into the 2-degree curve at MP 102 with an eastbound train as it departs Meadville Yard in August 1967. Soon the train will be clear of the 20 MPH speed restriction through downtown Meadville and will be cruising at the 50 MPH maximum. In the background are the former Atlantic & Great Western RR shops that the EL utilized as M-of-W shops. Other smaller shops were also housed in this complex such as the Sign Shop, the Air Brake Shop, the Test Lab, and others. Usually a substantial collection of M-of-W machinery could be found here as well as retired switching locomotives waiting to have their air brake control valves removed before being scrapped.

(ELHS Archives Collection)

RIGHT • A former Lackawanna Alco, RS3 #1043 hauls Train #37, the Jamestown – Meadville wayfreight between Cambridge Springs and Venango. Trains #38/37 operated six days a week between Meadville and Jamestown switching local industries along the route. The two boxcars behind the locomotive were pulled from Carnation Company at Cambridge Springs, PA.
(ELHS Archives Collection)

ABOVE • At Mill Village, PA the eastbound and westbound mains are separated by about 1000 yards. This westbound train rolls through the northwestern Pennsylvania countryside in the early spring of 1974. F7a #7124 leads a GP35 and an SDP45 with a mixed train to be switched at Meadville. The crew will be home for dinner with only about 25 miles to go before reaching it. *(William F. Herrmann, ELHS Archives Collection)*

LEFT • Recently abandoned, the 100-year-old station at Union City, PA in this 1973 photo is in its final year before demolition. In addition to handling LCL freight, the agent also handled the inbound and outbound shipments from Cherry Hill Lumber, Tru-Temper Tools and the PRR interchange. After the Agent was removed a few years earlier, the M-of-W and Signal Department used the building as their headquarters until it was razed in October 1973. *(William F. Herrmann, ELHS Archives Collection)*

RIGHT • A section of Train 100 hauled by SD45 #3625 and GP35 #2572 approaches Concord Street in Union City, PA in March 1973. The sidetrack to the right once served the Cherry Hill Lumber Division of Ethan-Allen Furniture Company. Nearly out of sight and ahead of the train is the Union City Hardwood Division of Tru-Temper Corp. Both industries were Erie Lackawanna customers.
(Ron Rohrbaugh, ELHS Archives Collection)

ABOVE • Train #7, THE PACIFIC EXPRESS, is passing the Railway Express Building as it slows for the station stop at Corry, PA in this circa 1964 view. The train, heavy with head-end work, was allowed about four minutes for station work at Corry. The train was down to a single coach as far as passenger accommodations were concerned, but they also had time for a quick light meal in the station restaurant at Binghamton, Youngstown or Marion.
(William F. Herrmann, ELHS Archives Collection)

LEFT • It's a cold and dreary 1966 morning at Corry, PA as Train #2 makes its stop, but the interior lighting and the steam emitting from the rear makes the Tavern Lounge car look warm and inviting. The raised crossing gate to the far left of the photo protects the Center Street crossing on the P&E Division of the PRR, which itself crosses the EL at MS Tower at Corry. The towering stack in the background is that of the Ajax Foundry; an EL customer that is served off of the Hole Track east of MS Tower.
(William F. Herrmann, ELHS Archives Collection)

ABOVE • Alco RS3 #1052 waits in the clear in the Hole Track at Corry for a westbound to pass before #37 continues toward Meadville to complete its switching duties. In the consist of the wayfreight, behind the box car is a locomotive crane and idler that was moved to and from various work locations on local freight trains. The photographer is standing on the tail track that leads back into town north of the PC line and serves several industries including The Ajax Foundry Company. The white post in the ground near the front of the locomotive indicates the clearance point on the side track so as not to foul the main track. *(William G. Herrmann, ELHS Archives Collection)*

ABOVE • A pair of Alco Centuries leads an eastbound hotshot across First Street at Corry, PA in this 1972 photo. The track to the left of the train is #8, a short runaround track that extends west to EYE Tower. The eastbound signal at EYE Tower can be seen in the distance. The EL manned MS Tower while the PC manned EYE Tower where an industrial track crossed the EL main.

(William F. Herrmann, ELHS Archives Collection)

ABOVE • This 1968 view is looking eastward, showing the former PRR track crossing the EL at MS Tower and Maple Avenue road crossing within the interlocking. The next crossing, Pennsylvania Avenue, is nearly out of view at the curve.

The railcars on the siding to the left are in "The Hole Track" with the tail track extending back into town along the north side of the PRR. The operator at MS also controlled the Maple Avenue crossing gates on both railroads. *(William F. Herrmann, ELHS Archives Collection)*

ABOVE • The operator at MS Tower watches an eastbound pass through Corry on a winter day in 1971. The EL was known for mixing first and second generation motive power in addition to mixing builders in the consists. GP35 #2567 is teamed up with a

pair of EMD F7b units and an Alco Century. The EL and the PC lines cross at MS, as does Maple Avenue. Corry lies in the Lake Erie snowbelt and is the recipient of generous amounts of lake effect snow.

(William F. Herrmann, ELHS Archives Collection)

RIGHT • Black and yellow were still the freight colors when the photographer took this photo in 1963 at Lovells, PA. The 12-year-old F7a leads an eastbound train under the PRR's Oil City to Buffalo line just west of Gates Street at Corry. The bridge, abandoned and void of rail, still stands in 2011.
(William F. Herrmann, ELHS Archives Collection)

LEFT • A work train powered by Alco C425 #2461 occupies the westward main track at Corry, PA in this August 12, 1972 photo. In the consist is a locomotive crane as well as gondola and hopper cars that indicate that the train may be assisting in the installation or removal of a switch.
(ELHS Archives Collection)

BELOW • Engineer C. T. "Clarence" Woodruff takes a break from throttle duties as the fireman operates the locomotive at Corry.
(ELHS Archives Collection)

ABOVE • Passenger equipped GP7 #1405, bumped from commuter duties, is assigned to trains #38 and 37 between Meadville and Jamestown in August 1971. Seen westbound at Corry, PA, the local will work at Corry, Union City, Cambridge Springs and "the Brake Shoe" before arriving at Meadville.

Note the two sets of MU hoses on the former DL&W unit; the upper set for the former Erie 6SL brake equipment and the lower ones for the standard 24RL and 26L brake equipment. With the exception of certain Baldwin and Lima locomotives, the former DL&W passenger GP7s would MU with any El power. *(ELHS Archives Collection)*

LEFT • A pair of Alco C424s leads a GE U25b westbound through a six-degree curve between Maple Avenue and Center Street in Corry in 1971. The home signals for EYE Tower can be seen in the distance. *(William F. Herrmann, ELHS Archives Collection)*

BELOW • An early section of Train NY100 is eastbound passing EYE Tower at Corry, PA in 1972 behind a pair of Alco C424s in 1972. It's unusual power for this train in 1972, but it'll get the job done. EYE Tower is the single-level building behind the signal case. In addition to operating switches and signals at LOVE west of Corry, it also handled the signals where the industrial track crossed the EL at MP 61.40. *(William F. Herrmann, ELHS Archives Collection)*

ABOVE • Three units provide 10,800 HP to haul a heavy eastbound upgrade across First Avenue at Corry, PA in this 1972 photo. An interesting open-top piggyback load is tucked in behind the rear unit. The crossing watchman's shanty sets above the freight house and controls the gates at First Avenue.

(William F. Herrmann, ELHS Archives Collection)

BELOW • Train X3 is powered by a single U33c in this May 1973 photo at Corry. The train was a glorified local that operated between Hornell and Meadville. X-3 set off and picked up at Olean, Salamanca and Jamestown. The high and wide cars on the head-end appear to be from Air Preheater Company of Wellsville, NY.

(ELHS Archives Collection)

ABOVE • Alco RS3 #923 arrives at Corry on Train #38 on a dark winter day. Corry was the snowiest location on the EL main line, with over 225 inches received annually.

(William F. Herrmann, ELHS Archives Collection)

BELOW • SD45 #3624 and Alco C424 #2402 haul a westbound mixed freight train between Ashville and Watts Flats, NY. The dreary February 1972 weather is emphasized by the grimy locomotive consist. The train is most likely a section of train #77.

(David Shaw, ELHS Archives Collection)

ABOVE • The photographer didn't provide any details on the location of this photo but it's still a classic view of two fairly-new SD45-2s in the summer of 1973. The head brakeman is enjoying the sunshine from the second unit of what appears to be a section of train #99 approaching Watts Flats, NY. *(David Shaw, ELHS Archives Collection)*

BELOW • Alco RS3 #930 handles a respectable-sized Train #37 through Watts Flats, NY in May 1973. Note that the crew has the caboose tucked in the middle of the train for ease in switching operations, indicating that the cars behind the caboose are for Corry and Cambridge Springs. *(David Shaw ELHS Archives Collection)*

ABOVE • Four units producing 10,000 HP move an eastbound Buffalo Coal Train across Hunt Road as the photographer braves the cold from the overhead bridge at Big Tree Road just west of Lakewood, NY in February 1972. A unit coal train destined to Semet-Solvay Division of Allied Chemical Company at Harriet near Buffalo operated via EL about once a week where it was made into coke. Coke is still produced at that location by Tonawanda Coke Company.

(David Shaw, ELHS Archives Collection)

ABOVE • Here's another view of an eastbound at the same location in early spring 1976 behind a pair of 45's running elephant-style. The white milepost in the photo shows "S 40," indicating 40 miles west of Salamanca. In 2011, the line is single track at this location and the Hunt Road Crossing has been upgraded to protection by flashing lights and gates by the Western New York & Pennsylvania RR.

(David Shaw, ELHS Archives Collection)

ABOVE • A U25b is the power for today's #38 as it passes through Celoron just prior to arriving at Jamestown in October 1972. Celoron, located two miles west of Jamestown, was the childhood home of actress Lucille Ball. Frequently, the power for the local was whatever was available in Meadville that particular morning.

Train and engine service employees were paid on a mileage basis and generally, 100 miles was a day's pay. Trains #38/37 operated six days a week and covered approximately 144 miles per day, so it paid quite well. *(David Shaw, ELHS Archives Collection)*

ABOVE • Train CX99 has plenty of power today as four "45s" haul the train westward through Celoron, NY in August 1971. A total of 14,400 HP will guarantee Joe Lifschultz's freight will be on time at Chicago. *(David Shaw, ELHS Archives Collection)*

ABOVE • Caboose C207 clears Livingston Avenue at MP 36.07 in Celoron, NY as a westbound train continues its wintry weather trek to Meadville. It's January 1975 but someone has chalked a "CR" on the caboose side in anticipation of the future owner. The switch in the foreground on Track #2 leads to the Eastern Plywood Company. *(David Shaw, ELHS Archives Collection)*

ABOVE • The engineer of an eastbound looks back at his train as it passes through Jamestown at MP 33.50. The track on the lower level leads to the Freight House. The main line through Jamestown is built on bridge-like structures and is filled with stone. *(David Shaw, ELHS Archives Collection)*

LEFT • SDP45 #3647 leads Delaware & Hudson Alco C628 #612 westbound through the Jamestown Station with train Advance NY99 in April 1973. The big Alco units were a familiar sight on EL but not usually on hotshot trains such as the 99s. The Jamestown Furniture Exposition Mart towers above the station in this photo. *(David Shaw, ELHS Archives Collection)*

ABOVE • Former DL&W Alco road switcher #1042 idles on the Second Street Spur on a frigid January 1971 Jamestown morning. The stack and building behind the locomotive was the steam heat plant, operated by the Erie RR to provide steam and hot water for the station, yard office and diesel shop.

The Jamestown area has always favored hot water heat and the city's Board of Public Utilities presently has a Central Heating Facility. Much of the downtown area is served by a hot water heating system operated by the Samuel A. Carlson Generating Station.

(David Shaw, ELHS Archives Collection)

ABOVE • GP7 #1219 departs westbound from Jamestown, NY with Train #37, the Jamestown to Meadville wayfreight on August 21, 1974. Jamestown was a city of diverse industry with most of it located on the Erie Lackawanna Railroad.

The plant in the background, Automatic Registering Machine Corporation, manufactured automatic voting machines and is still in business under a new name. *(David Shaw, ELHS Archives Collection)*

ABOVE • In this undated photo, we see a cut of five freshly painted M-of-W camp cars at Jamestown. The cut of cars has a caboose on the end so it is probably train HF98 that has pulled in the clear to work while allowing other trains to pass. The cars are destined for Salamanca, which was the headquarters of a system Carpenter Gang and a system Bridge Gang. *(David Shaw, ELHS Archives Collection)*

RIGHT • A "Lite engine," which is a term used for a locomotive when it is operated without a train, can occur for several reasons. It could be to pick up a train at a certain location or to move excess motive power from one point to another, but it could also be to balance a crew pool. Many times a lite section was ordered from Hornell to Meadville on a Monday when westbound traffic was virtually non-existent. A pair of "45s" is seen as they pass the Jamestown Diesel Shop at the permitted 30 MPH in October 1973. *(ELHS Archives Collection)*

ABOVE • Looking west from the Third Street Viaduct, an eastbound train behind SD45-2 #3666 breaks through the morning sunlight in November 1975. The boxcar to the right rests on track JN-1, and the facing point lead going out of the photo to the right is the old Jamestown, Westfield & Northwestern RR, of which the Erie acquired about a mile of track in town after the JWNW ceased operations. *(David Shaw, ELHS Archives Collection)*

ABOVE • In the previous chapter we saw a photo of a weed burner/snow melter at Meadville. We see a similar machine at work cleaning the switches at Second Street in December 1972. For the most part, the machines were only used in the yard since the fuel oil and flames were not kind to bond wires and switch insulation found on the main tracks. *(David Shaw, ELHS Archives Collection)*

RIGHT • Generally overlooked by photographers and railfans but sought after by modelers are photos of such items such as this fueling station at Jamestown, NY, seen in June 1971. The near-standard railroad version of a gas pump, the SERV-A-TRAIN is shown alongside the filter system.

(ELHS Archives Collection)

BELOW • By the early 1970s second-generation motive power was beginning to show up on work trains, locals and even yard jobs. GP35 #2582 is at Jamestown in the late spring sunlight. Jamestown relied on the railroad to serve the many woodworking shops, furniture factories and other manufacturing plants. The warehouse of the Automatic Voting Machine Company can be seen in this photo. AVM was an EL customer and had several plants and warehouses in town. *(David Shaw, ELHS Archives Collection)*

ABOVE • Erie Alco S4 #529, dressed in black, adds a solemn look to this May 1965 photo. It's complemented by the drab green of the station passageways, and the weathered brick of the station and annex building.

(David Shaw, ELHS Archives Collection)

RIGHT • Seven years later, during the summer of 1972, former Erie Railroad Alco S4 #529, still in black and yellow and still lettered ERIE, was again working Jamestown Yard. We're fortunate that the photographer captured this image of the Alco-GE builder's plate attached to the locomotive.

(David Shaw, ELHS Archives Collection)

BELOW • In a rather generic April 1974 view of a westbound local at Jamestown we get a good look at the action end of the Diesel Shop. The shop held one switcher model locomotive and could be accessed from the west end only. The smaller door, the one without damage from a locomotive stack when not opened entirely, was for M-of-W Department trucks. The sand tower was a "one of a kind" as far as we know. A Structures Department car is behind the shop. The building remains, as of this writing, as a M-of-W and Signal Department storage building for the Western New York & Pennsylvania Railroad. *(David Shaw, ELHS Archives Collection)*

AMERICAN LOCOMOTIVE CO.
GENERAL ELECTRIC CO.
SCHENECTADY, N.Y.
80090
OCTOBER
1952

ABOVE • In this June 1973 photo we see the east end of the Diesel Shop, which contained the trainmen's welfare room, yard office (housing the General Yardmaster and clerk) and also offices and storage for the Mechanical and M-of-W Department.

(David Shaw, ELHS Archives Collection)

ABOVE • A beehive of activity is taking place near the Second Street Crossovers in this February 1973 midday photo. The Jamestown Yard crew is holding in the clear along the Chadakoin River while the crew of the Meadville to Jamestown Local, #38, backs their train in the yard. GP7 #1272 is ready to make a move to get the outbound cars for #138, the B&SW Local.

(David Shaw, ELHS Archives Collection)

ABOVE • EMD SW8 #365 pulls up from the Shermans Hole Track, locally known as the Hill Track, into the Second Street Yard and will tie onto coal in the Main Street Yard and take it to the Jamestown City Light Plant in April 1973. City Light was a steady customer and received a half-dozen cars of coal six days a week. *(David Shaw, ELHS Archives Collection)*

RIGHT • Faded and dirty but still reliable to handle daily switching chores, Alco S2 #506 was a regularly assigned locomotive during the early 1970s. During the 1960s the Baldwin switchers were a Jamestown standard, followed by the Alco S series in the early '70s and then the EMD SW8 and larger models in the mid-70's. Engine #506 is spotted on the Second Street Spur in this December 1972 photo. *(David Shaw, ELHS Archives Collection)*

ABOVE • Seen just prior to the end of the Baldwin era at Jamestown, a model DS4-4-1000 #612 handles the yard duties in a January 1971 snowstorm. The plant in the background is the Samuel A. Carlson Generating Station of Jamestown City Light Company, presently known as the Jamestown Board of Public Utilities. The plant is a twin unit plant capable of producing 53.7 Megawatts of electricity.

(David Shaw, ELHS Archives Collection)

BELOW • A month later, the venerable Eddystone product, still carrying its Erie lettering, is noted with makeshift shutters placed on the front of the locomotive to assist it in maintaining proper operating temperature. The strong west winds from Lake Chautauqua made Jamestown a frigid location in the winter.

(David Shaw, ELHS Archives Collection)

LEFT • Trains BM7, BM9, MF74 and HF98 that operated between Meadville and Buffalo frequently drew a quartet of EMD GP7s. Train MF74 is in a January 1970 blizzard as it arrives in Jamestown, which was a common site there in the winter. Thankfully, the photographer braved the elements to capture this classic photo. *(Ron Rohrbaugh, ELHS Archives Collection)*

BELOW • As many industries removed their sidetracks and the railroads reduced the number of public team tracks, receivers of freight had to revert to locations and methods such as this for inbound shipments. This Seaboard Coast Line boxcar is unloaded on the Lower Show Track at Jamestown in January 1973. *(David Shaw, ELHS Archives Collection)*

RIGHT • An unidentified east-bound drifts downgrade as it leaves Jamestown and enters Falconer in February 1971. The lake effect snow definitely kept the M-of-W active during the winter in this area! *(David Shaw, ELHS Archives Collection)*

RIGHT • Buffalo engineer Frank Joyce gives a wave to the photographer from the cab of Cadillac #1263. The six GP9s were nicknamed "Cadillacs" by all as they were the pride of the fleet and the highest horsepower freight locomotives on the Erie Railroad when purchased in 1956. Frank was an engineer on the South Dayton to Jamestown wayfreight in this August 1973 photo and always was a jovial person with which to work.
(David Shaw, ELHS Archives Collection)

LEFT • Brakeman Jim Miller keeps an eye on the photographer at Jamestown in August 1972 as the yard crew waits in the clear for a move by the B&SW Local. Mr. Miller will tie the C424 #2406 onto outbound train #138 and depart for South Dayton, NY. *(David Shaw, ELHS Archives Collection)*

BELOW • A pair of E8s and an F unit make a setoff in the Main Street Yard at Jamestown in October 1972. The E units were used frequently on trains HF98 and X-3 between Meadville and Hornell, stopping to work at Jamestown, Salamanca and Olean, NY. *(David Shaw, ELHS Archives Collection)*

ABOVE • Train #38, the local from Meadville, is making a move on their train at the Second Street crossover before departure in April 1974. The Alco RS3 #932 will tie onto the west end of the track and depart Jamestown for the 74-mile return trip.

(David Shaw, ELHS Archives Collection)

BELOW • A splash of fall color is in view in this down-on shot of Alco C425 #2452 in October 1972 as the crew moves east to Main Street to do their work. The yard crew with S2 #517 has completed the pickup for the train and will stay in the clear at Second Street.

(David Shaw, ELHS Archives Collection)

ABOVE • The Advance-CX99 passes through Jamestown with a pair of GP35 in this April 1973 photo. The Carlson Generating Station of Jamestown City Light forms the backdrop for this photo. A few employees "shoot the bull" at the shop building. The track between the shop and the westbound main is known as the Second Street Spur. *(David Shaw, ELHS Archives Collection)*

LEFT • An eastbound, most likely NY100, has business car #3 behind the caboose passing through Jamestown in March 1974. Car #3 was assigned to R. F. Bush, Chief Engineer, and was equipped with a Baker-Prestone heater and was self-sufficient as far as heat and lighting were concerned. *(David Shaw, ELHS Archives Collection)*

LEFT • A crewmember stands in front of the yard office portion of the station basement as the Advance-CX99 passes with a single SD45-2. The Advance section of the Croxton 99 was usually a light but fast train. A single SD or a pair of GP35s was sufficient power. Noontime in Jamestown was a busy time with multiple sections of train 99, a yard crew and a B&SW local in the area. This locomotive lasted through the Conrail era and was passed to CSX as #8973 in the Conrail acquisition of 1999. *(David Shaw, ELHS Archives Collection)*

ABOVE • There are a couple of interesting items in this next series of photos. An inspection train on the line makes a stop in Jamestown in August 1973. Jamestown was hardly a major source of revenue for the EL at that time and there were no division-level offices located in Jamestown by that date. Additionally, the special train is lead by E8a #831 rather than the usual #833.

*(David Shaw,
ELHS Archives Collection)*

RIGHT • The engine crew takes a break prior to departure.

*(David Shaw,
ELHS Archives Collection)*

RIGHT • *Spirit of Youngstown*, a 1954-built, 10-roomette, five-double-bedroom sleeping car provided a place for the train crew to ride as well as additional sleeping space for the guests, porters and waiters on the business cars. The *Spirit* was conveyed to Conrail as Car #11, where it served the entire Conrail era in Office Car Special service.

*(David Shaw,
ELHS Archives Collection)*

LEFT • Business Car #2 was assigned to the Vice President—Operations and was built for the Central Railroad of New Jersey in April 1930. It was acquired by the Erie RR in June 1936.
(ELHS Archives Collection)

LEFT • Bringing up the markers is EL Business Car #300, a former Delaware & Hudson car that arrived on the EL with President William White. It previously was a NYC car when White was with the Central. *(David Shaw, ELHS Archives Collection)*

BELOW • In this view we see the train departing Jamestown. *(David Shaw, ELHS Archives Collection)*

RIGHT • The conductor of train MF74 grabs his copy of the train orders on the fly from the operator at DV Tower, Falconer, NY in July 1972. The train has just crossed over to #1 track to operate to Waterboro where it will enter the B&SW Branch. One of the former Erie Railroad's machine operator's trailers can be seen in the photo. These trailers were used to house employees who operated bulldozers, cranes and other M-of-W equipment while away from home. *(David Shaw, ELHS Archives Collection)*

RIGHT, CENTER • It's a wet July morning in 1971 as SD45 #3615 leads a westbound under the Work Street Bridge at Falconer, NY. Note the difference in the dwarf signals in the photo. The eastward signal on the westward track is a searchlight type while the signal from the siding is a position-light type signal. The latter type was usually associated with the Pennsylvania Railroad and is a rarity on EL.

(David Shaw, ELHS Archives Collection)

BELOW • A pair of F units hauls an eastbound HF98 through Falconer, NY in May 1972. Falconer is the site of the New York Central's DAV&P Branch crossing. The locomotive has just passed the eastbound home signal for DV Tower. The barricades protect the property from errant vehicles on Work Street, which has been relocated to an overhead bridge just out of view to the right. Another example of a Position Light Signal can be seen governing the route from the Old Main into the interlocking. Note the outside-braced, wooden boxcar behind the B unit, probably a Wellsville, Addison & Galeton RR car for the WAG interchange at Wellsville, NY.

(David Shaw, ELHS Archives Collection)

ABOVE • U25B #2504 handles wrecking derrick #03302 and wreck train at DV Tower, Falconer, NY in July 1972. It appears that the train is being switched in order to shove to the derailment with the derrick first out. The derrick, a 250-ton capacity Industrial-Brownhoist, was one of three of that size on the EL and was assigned at Meadville and Brier Hill at various periods. DV Tower stands to the right and the NYC crossing can be seen in the photo. The overhead structure is the Work Street Bridge, erected in the 1950s to eliminate a dangerous crossing at grade. *(David Shaw, ELHS Archives Collection)*

ABOVE • This is a view of the rear of derrick #03302 and idler car under the Work Street Bridge. *(David Shaw, ELHS Archives Collection)*

ABOVE • A Speno Rail Grinding train is tied up for the weekend on the Second Street Spur in Jamestown in February 1973. The passenger cars behind U25b #2510 are the living quarters for the Speno operators. Following those cars is the power car that provides electricity for the grinding wheels on the trailing cars. The train is equipped with over a hundred grinding wheels that restore the proper railhead contour as it moves along at 6 MPH. A telephone cable is rigged alongside the locomotive so the grinding crew can communicate with the engine crew.

(David Shaw,
ELHS Archives Collection)

RIGHT, CENTER • In this view across the Chadakoin River, Alco S2 #517 spots a cut of coal over the unloading pit at the Jamestown City Light Plant in November 1972. The rail spur was originally part of the Jamestown, Chautauqua & Lake Erie RR and was acquired by the Erie Railroad. Most of the coal for City Light originated on the Erie's Bradford Division.

(David Shaw,
ELHS Archives Collection)

RIGHT • The Jamestown mechanical forces are replacing a pair of wheels on a freight car truck in March 1973. In many instances, work at outlying points was performed in this primitive manner. *(David Shaw,*
ELHS Archives Collection)

ABOVE • While derailments are always costly and result in traffic delays, this minor mishap on August 17, 1975 was a lucky break for EL. A handful of cars in the consist of an eastbound train derailed to the south, resulting in the westbound main track being clear to run trains. The yard crew is working with an SW8 locomotive with the Jamestown City Light plant in the background.

The insulated pipes that cross the Chadakoin River are for the District Hot Water Heating system in downtown Jamestown. The passageway from the depot to the platforms is boarded up and will be removed in the next year or so by Conrail. The green color is a result of the copper covering. The westbound (far) side of the walkway was equipped with an escalator. *(David Shaw, ELHS Archives Collection)*

ABOVE • Here's a close-up view of the derailment. *(David Shaw, ELHS Archives Collection)*

RIGHT • A westbound kicks up the fresh snow in this February 1971 photo from the Work Street Bridge at Falconer. The long #15 crossovers at Falconer permitted 30 MPH when crossing over from one track to the other. The tower and the maintainer's headquarters are divided by the Dunkirk, Allegheny Valley & Pittsburgh Branch crossing at MP 30.65. The Jamestown area was subjected to large amounts of "lake effect" snowfall produced by both Lake Erie and nearby Chautauqua Lake. *(David Shaw, ELHS Archives Collection)*

ABOVE • Train NY99 approaches the switch leading to 84 Lumber Company at Kennedy, NY in late spring 1975. The train is on what was originally the B&SW RR main between Waterboro and Falconer, NY. Advertised running time between Salamanca and Meadville was two hours and 40 minutes, with actual running time frequently about 20 minutes less than that. *(David Shaw, ELHS Archives Collection)*

BELOW • Following NY99 closely at Kennedy, NY is SC99 en route from Scranton to Chicago. The late-morning sun nicely illuminates the underside of the SD45, SDP45 and an unidentified Alco Century. Train SC99 contained a mixture of freight from Scranton and Binghamton and empty freight cars returning to the west such as the center-beam and bulkhead flat cars in this photo.

(David Shaw, ELHS Archives Collection)

ABOVE • Freshly-painted GP7 #1201 and a similar caboose are on the Team Track at Kennedy, NY in August 1971. The power is probably assigned to a work train, and hopefully it's a weed spray train. Note the barrel style headlight on the locomotive; only #1200 and 1201 were so equipped. *(ELHS Archives Collection)*

ABOVE • RH Tower, located at MP S14.0 between Randolph and Steamburg, NY, is the beginning of the double track eastbound to Salamanca. The view appears to be from the rear of a westbound train showing the switch from #1 to the single track still in the reverse position. The location is controlled by the "DX" Train Dispatcher in Youngstown, OH. This 1974 photo shows, left to right, a shanty for an operator when required for maintenance purposes, the CIL (Central Instrument Location) to control the switch and signals and propane tanks to fuel the switch heaters in the winter.

(Ron Rohrbaugh, ELHS Archives Collection)

RIGHT • Train MF74 in charge of F3a #8054 pulls from the Buffalo & Southwestern Branch #2 track and crosses the former Nickel Plate Road tracks at BC Jct. in south Buffalo, NY. The train is entering the Buffalo Creek Railroad's property for the final few miles of its 140-mile run from Meadville, PA to Bison Yard. This location is the furthest north-eastern end of the Mahoning Division. The EL's practice of mixing EMD and Alco products is noted with Alco FB1 #7313 as the second unit in the consist. The N&W's Tifft Street Yard is in the background.

(Ron Rohrbaugh, ELHS Archives Collection)

ABOVE • Westbound train BM9 with second generation power is approaching BC Jct. on the eastbound Buffalo Creek RR track as it prepares to pick up orders from the Operator at BC to enter the B&SW Branch. The train orders originated from the "DX" train dispatcher in Youngstown, OH, which controls the track west of this location. The moves at BC Jct. are restricted to 10 MPH, and the vertical position of the target gives trains on the Buffalo Creek permission to cross the Norfolk & Western RR. The overhead rail line in the background is the EL's City Branch. The N&W locomotive in the photo is on the N&W-BCK transfer track. The location is a busy one with drawbridges, targets, switches, crossing frogs and even some hand-operated movable point frogs! The ground is surprisingly void of snow in this February 1967 photo.

(Ron Rohrbaugh, ELHS Archives Collection)

LEFT • Trains BM9 (left) and MF74 (right) meet at BC Jct. in February 1967. Coming off the Buffalo Creek RR BM9 will operate in double track for ¾ of a mile, passing the MF74, and enter the single track at the spring switch located at MP 3.52. BM9's power and braking capacity will be severely tested 27 miles south of here when descending the 2.7-mile, 1.25% grade to Gowanda and then climbing the 4.6-mile, 2.72% grade to DM Junction. Gowanda Hill was the Erie's steepest Main Line grade.

(Ron Rohrbaugh, ELHS Archives Collection)

ABOVE • Train MF74 (Meadville to Buffalo) has cleared BC Jct. and the BM9 behind a mixed Alco-EMD consist is ready to depart to Meadville. The train will make a set-off at Gowanda for the Hi-Di Local and will pick up Meadville cars at Jamestown. *(Ron Rohrbaugh, ELHS Archives Collection)*

LEFT • BM9 is departing the BC Drawbridge with a "normal" EL locomotive consist: FA1, F3b, F3b, and an RS3. The 6100 HP consist will have its work cut out for it on the B&SW. *(Ron Rohrbaugh, ELHS Archives Collection)*

BELOW • The former NKP drawbridge is to the left of the BCK bridge and the NKP – BCK transfer track or connection is to the extreme left. The yellow pedestal signal indicates that the drawbridge is down and locked and the train may proceed. *(Ron Rorhbaugh, ELHS Archives Collection)*

SALAMANCA TO HORNELL INCLUDING DUNKIRK AND BRADFORD BRANCHES

As stated in the previous chapter, Salamanca to Hornell was formerly known as the Allegany Division until 1962 when it was merged into the Mahoning Division as the 4th Sub-Division. Until 1962 Salamanca was a Division Headquarters with a Superintendent, Division Engineer, Train Dispatchers and other staff to supervise the division. The offices were eliminated in 1962 except for the Trainmaster and the Road Foreman of Engines. The Train Dispatchers were relocated to Youngstown and the switching yard was closed except for one nightly yard crew. Salamanca remained the home terminal for the daily wayfreight to Dunkirk and the daily freight train to Brockway, PA on the Bradford Division that met the main line at Carrollton, just a few miles east of Salamanca.

Salamanca to Olean was double track, Automatic Block Signal territory and the line ran along the Allegheny River for most of the way to Olean. At Olean, X Tower, manned by EL operators, was the location of the PRR's Harrisburg to Buffalo Line crossing. An active interchange between the EL and the PRR remained in place right up to Conrail. The few industries located on the EL at Olean were served by the Wellsville Wayfreight.

East of Olean the line climbed gently from the river valley to CB Jct. near Cuba, NY where the line split with the Old Main Line running to the southeast through Cuba, Friendship, Belmont, Belvidere, Wellsville, Andover, Alfred and Almond before dropping into Hornell. This Old Main Line had ruling grades of about 1% in both directions at two locations, Summit and Tip Top.

The alternate route from CB Jct and the favored route for heavy freight trains pre-Conrail was the River Line from CB Jct to River Jct and the Buffalo Division Main Line from River Jct to Hornell. The mileage via the River Line/Buffalo Division was 59.4 miles vs. 52.6 miles via the Old Main Line. The River Line was CTC and the Buffalo Division was Automatic Block Signals while the Old Main Line was a series of very short sidings, usable only to meet the wayfreight and passenger trains with Absolute Permissive Block (APB) signaling.

The Dunkirk Branch was a continuation of the main line from New York to the original end of the Erie RR at the Lake Erie port town. Into EL years, the Dunkirk Branch was still being used for unit coal trains off of the B&O at Salamanca and from the Bradford Division. The coal was destined to the Niagara Mohawk's Dunkirk Generating Station served by the NYC. Other shippers on the line included the Dunkirk locomotive plant of Alco and several feed and grain elevators. The Dunkirk Branch crossed the B&SW Branch at Dayton, NY on an archway that resembled a short tunnel. The arch was a clearance issue for trains on the B&SW. The EL interchanged with the NYC and the Nickel Plate at Dunkirk. A daily local operated from Salamanca to Dunkirk and back but after a series of slides and washouts occurred in the early 1970s, the track was removed from service between Cattaraugus and Dayton and the Dunkirk Wayfreight reported for duty at Dayton working west to Dunkirk. At another point in time, trains #241 & 240 reported for duty at Dayton.

The Bradford Branch, previously known as the Bradford Division, was a confusing operation of former Erie and B&O trackage between Limestone and Bradford. The Bradford Branch began at Carrollton, NY with the crews working out of Salamanca. The EL owned the line from Carrollton, NY through Limestone to Lewis Run, PA, a distance of 17.2 miles. A wayfreight known as the Lewis Run Turn worked from Salamanca to Lewis Run and return daily, handling mostly chores at the refineries at Bradford, PA. A five-day-a-week westbound freight train operated via the EL from Salamanca to Limestone, where it entered B&O trackage for the run to Erie Jct, near Brockway, PA, returning eastward the following day. At Brockway, the EL interchanged with the PRR and the Pittsburg & Shawmut, receiving unit coal trains from the P&S on a near-daily basis.

BELOW • For the most part, Salamanca Yard was switched by an EMD SW8 locomotive that was shared by the daylight Lewis Run Turn and the nighttime yard crew. This unit, classed SE-8 (switcher, EMD, 800 HP), was new to the Lackawanna as #511. The sweet little "pup" is on the enginehouse lead at Salamanca on May 28, 1973 next to an unusual high and wide shipment.

LEFT • General Electric U25b #2527, the last of the model ordered by EL, is on the service track at Salamanca, NY in 1965. The unit was covering the Brockway Local that operated between Salamanca, NY and Brockway, PA. *(William F. Herrmann, ELHS Archives Collection)*

LEFT • With the advent of Conrail, some of the SW8 locomotives were sold or assigned to New Jersey Transit for yard work at Hoboken, Elizabethport, and other locations. This resulted in Salamanca losing its favorite unit. In this photo, SW1200 #456, the replacement "pup" is on the yard lead at the "subway" on May 13, 1976. The former BR&P Salamanca Passenger Station sits directly behind the unit. *(Ron Rohrbaugh, ELHS Archive Collection)*

BELOW • A very nicely lighted photo of Alco RS3 #915 shows off the fuel and water tanks, the air reservoir, the trucks, wheels, sander hoses, brake assembly and the speed indicator/recorder cable. The remains of the coaling station and sanding towers can be seen in the photo. The Salamanca hillside is quite bare in this November 18, 1973 photo. *(Ron Rohrbaugh, ELHS Archives Collection)*

ABOVE • Salamanca was the home terminal for Train #241, the Dunkirk Way Freight, as well as the Brockway Extra. This photo, taken on October 8, 1971, shows a set of F-units, led by F7a #6321 on-hand for the 10:00 AM on-duty time for the RYX train to Brockway. At this time, there were two crews working in the Bradford Division pool: one departing Salamanca on Sunday, Tuesday and Thursday and returning the following days, and another departing on Monday, Wednesday and Friday. The normal trip south, or west as noted in the timetable, was empties with return trip consisting of mainly coal for Dunkirk, Buffalo, or the B&O at Salamanca.

(Ron Rohrbaugh, ELHS Archives Collection)

LEFT • Three weeks later, on October 29, 1971 the photographer captured this late afternoon arrival of the Bradford Division train at Salamanca, led by sister unit #6331. The frost has taken its toll on the foliage in Cattaraugus County and soon "Old Man Winter" would be upon us—again.

(Ron Rohrbaugh, ELHS Archives Collection)

LEFT • Salamanca's locomotive department at the time of this photo on May 6, 1973 consisted of a foreman, an electrician and two laborers. Their main duties were to fuel east and westbound through trains at the main track fueling stations. The fuel stations were located where no road crossings would be blocked during the operation and it eliminated the crossing issue at Meadville and a much larger issue at Hornell: returning to the diesel shop for fuel. The forces also serviced the power for the yard crew and the local trains that were home terminal at Salamanca. Additionally, the HF98 or X3 power would be placed at the shop after yarding the train. A late-model F3a #7104 mated with an SD45 was most likely the power for HF98 this date while the Brockway Extra (RYX) power rested in the background.
(ELHS Archives Collection)

ABOVE • Erie Lackawanna often mixed locomotives without regard to model or builder. In this April 1972 photo at Salamanca we see second-generation models from GE, EMD and Alco present along with a first-generation EMD in the consist. Even at this date, the Salamanca service track was a fairly busy place with the Dunkirk Local, the Brockway Local, the Yard Job and X3 and HF98's power arriving. *(ELHS Archives Collection)*

LEFT • It's October 19, 1972 and frost has already kissed the hardwood forest lining the north side of Salamanca, NY. EMD F7b #7133 is mated with Alco RS2 #907 on the service track as the outbound power for train X-3. The glorified local will be on duty at 8:00 PM to switch the yard and work towards Meadville with a stop at Jamestown. *(Ron Rohrbaugh, ELHS Archives Collection)*

ABOVE • Looking back from the fireman's seat of an eastbound train we get a great view of the east end of Salamanca Yard in August 1972.

The redbrick structure on the right is the B&O's (former BR&P) Salamanca Passenger Station. Salamanca was home to two separate stations on the B&O: Salamanca and East Salamanca. Additionally, the EL and the PRR had stations in town. *(ELHS Archives Collection)*

LEFT • Wellsville, NY was the reporting location for Second Class Train #281, a wayfreight that operated between Andover and Olean, NY. GP9 #1265, one of the former Erie's six "Cadillacs," is seen in this August 1971 photo. Wellsville was a source of high revenue traffic with excessive dimension loads out of Air Preheater Corp. Other industries in town included a lumber yard, a turbine manufacturer and, of course, the interchange with the Wellsville, Addison & Galeton RR. The WPA-style building in the background is the U. S. Post Office building, still in use today. *(Ron Rohrbaugh, ELHS Archives Collection)*

LEFT, CENTER • Erie 464015 is a camp car assigned to the operator of Locomotive Crane 2909. When the crane was assigned to a work location, the crane, idler and camp car were spotted for use on a house track or camp car track where water and electricity was available. The operator of the locomotive crane would use the camp car to live in and as an office. One operator was usually assigned to one specific crane and camp car for the season. In this July 1985 photo we see the car spotted along Rochester Street in Salamanca, NY, and it's now the property of the Salamanca Railroad Museum.
(Mike Kopach, ELHS Archives Collection)

BELOW • Hornell was the home shop for most 1st generation GM locomotives including this GP7 #1242. The unit is a rather nondescript standard GP7 without dynamic brakes. It was built with wiring and provisions for the addition of Automatic Train Stop (ATS), but ATS was removed from service on the EL prior to this photo being taken in July 1965. A standard Erie concrete phone booth and a locomotive tender are in the photo.
(Ron Rohrbaugh, ELHS Archives Collection)

Right • A one-of-a-kind paint scheme is seen on F7b #6112 at Hornell on March 14, 1976. The 1949-built EMD received this unique coat of paint in November 1975 and was noted in the dead line at Marion in January 1976. The 1500 HP unit was assigned Conrail #3850, but there is no evidence of it ever carrying that number or operating under Conrail. The unit was later seen in storage at Altoona on August 28, 1976. Retired Hornell shop worker Dick Welles indicated that the unit was painted in this scheme at Scranton or more likely, Marion. A Baldwin six-axle truck is on a flatcar in this photo. *(F. D. Tempesta, ELHS Archives Collection)*

Right • EMD SW8 #366 is at Hornell Shop on July 7, 1974 appearing a bit shabby, and the property doesn't look too well maintained, either. The unit is one of three orders placed by the DL&W for a total of eleven of the 800 HP units. *(ELHS Archives Collection)*

Below • Three former DL&W EMD F7a units: #6361, #6321 and #6341 are in storage at Hornell Shop on January 15, 1976. The units would be conveyed to Conrail in three months and would operate again for the new company out of Cleveland, carrying #1884, #1880 and #1882, respectively. *(ELHS Archives Collection)*

ABOVE • Alco RS3 #932, covered with oil and grime, is at Hornell in May 1975. A collection of Structures Department camp cars are in the distance along with derrick #03138.

Wrecker #03138 was a 160-ton capacity, steam-powered Bucyrus-Erie machine purchased in 1929 and assigned to Pt. Jervis.

(ELHS Archives Collection)

ABOVE • A trio of GP35s passes the Hornell Station, which also housed the Susquehanna Division Offices in this July 1965 photo. In less than a mile the train will reach Cass Street interlocking where the line splits, allowing the passenger trains and selected freight trains to operate via the Old Main Line to CB Jct, or trains could turn northerly on the Buffalo Line and access the Mahoning Division via the River Line at River Jct. Since there is no Operator present to hand up train orders, this train is going to Buffalo Division.

(Ron Rohrbaugh, ELHS Archives Collection)

RIGHT • Former Lackawanna GP7 #1275 sits on the ready track at Hornell Shop on July 7, 1974. A member of the EMD Class of 1952, the unit carried DL&W #956 and much later was assigned Conrail #5990. Some of the shop buildings can be seen in this photo. Hornell Shop is alive and well today, owned and operated by Alstom. *(Ron Rohrbaugh, ELHS Archives Collection)*

ABOVE • With lunch being over, the crew of train #241 with GP9 #1261 and caboose C149 prepare to make a move at Dayton, NY in June 1974. At Dayton, the Dunkirk Branch crosses over the top of the B&SW Branch on what is known as the Dayton Arch. The station served both the Dunkirk Branch and the B&SW Branch but was located on the former since it was the original Erie RR main line. Cars for the Dunkirk Local were ferried to DM Jct by trains on the B&SW and moved via the transfer track to the Dunkirk Branch. *(ELHS Archives Collection)*

RIGHT • A pair of nearly-new SD45-2's stops at East Avenue Hornell for a crew change on August 5, 1973. Soon the units will be hauling the westbound train up the Buffalo Division or over the Old Main Line. *(Ron Rohrbaugh, ELHS Archives Collection)*

While Buffalo proper was not part of the Mahoning Division it is covered briefly in this book due to the method of operations to and from Buffalo. Four daily freight trains operated between Buffalo and Meadville. The Buffalo & Southwestern Branch, formerly a Division itself, ran southwest from Buffalo to Jamestown.

The EL was a partner with the Nickel Plate Road in the building of a modern multi-million dollar classification yard in Buffalo known as Bison Yard. While labor issues prevented the NKP from using the yard, it was a joint operation with N&W after 1964. Bison Yard was also the location for major interchange with the former Wabash and Chesapeake & Ohio lines that operated through Ontario.

Crews from Meadville operated directly to Buffalo's Bison Yard via the B&SW Branch in one direction, returning the following day via the Buffalo Division at River Jct.

ABOVE • Baldwin power was a norm on the Mahoning Division whether it be yard or local service. The Baldwin DRS66-1500s were assigned at Brier Hill, Salamanca and/or Buffalo for most of their careers hauling coal or ore. DRS66-1500 #1158 was a local favorite at Brier Hill and was equipped with dynamic brakes. In this July 12, 1970 photo, the unit is assigned at Bison Yard in Buffalo. *(Mike Tedesco, ELHS Archives Collection)*

RIGHT • Alco switchers (and road-switchers as well) were rare EL items in Buffalo. Buffalo was EMD stomping grounds as far as switchers were concerned after the Baldwin units were sent west to Youngstown and later retired. Alco S2 #548 is on the caboose track at Bison Yard on December 22, 1974. The unit was sold by EL to Naporano Iron & Metal Company of Newark, NJ in 1972 but was resold by NI&M to locomotive dealer George Silcott of Worthington, OH in 1974. The unit in this photo was being moved to Silcott's yard for some mechanical work before it was resold to Chapparal Steel in Midlothian, TX. *(ELHS Archives Collection)*

BELOW • A pair of Baldwin model DR66-1500 units sets on the Bison Yard Service Track in this September 1968 photo. Buffalo was a haven for the four-axle Baldwin model AS16, but the six-axle units usually arrived from Hornell or Meadville and turned back to those locations. *(ELHS Archives Collection)*

Due to the volume of business on the Mahoning Division, much of it remained in service after Conrail acquired the Erie Lackawanna on April 1, 1976. While the preponderance of thru traffic was rerouted to former PRR and NYC lines, the industrial base on the division dictated that service of some nature was required. Much of the Mahoning Division was quickly downgraded by removing multiple track mains as well as eliminating unneeded yards and unused side tracks and, as soon as it was practical, signal systems were also removed and train speeds were reduced.

After millions of local, state and federal dollars, as well as money pledged by investors, the entire former Allegany and Meadville Divisions (the Mahoning Division's Fourth and Third sub-division as we know them) remain in service as the Western New York and Pennsylvania RR, LLC. The line, in addition to grasping for the remaining local freight service, also maintains the route used by NS unit coal and empty trains feeding the power plants of the Southern Tier of New York and southwestern New England. The WNYP also operates the former EL's Oil City Branch between Meadville and Oil City. The New York and Lake Erie operates the southern end of the B&SW between Gowanda and Conewango Valley and a portion of the Dunkirk Branch between Dayton and Cattaraugus. The Buffalo Southern is the designated operator from Buffalo to Gowanda. Other portions of the Mahoning Division did not fare as well. Norfolk Southern provides local service between Youngstown and Meadville with the Shenango Valley area remaining a bright spot for NS. The Second Sub-Division also remains in service from Latimer to North Warren as the NS's Niles Secondary Track. The Ohio Central, under former owner Jerry Joe Jacobson, purchased the Brier Hill Cluster in 1996, which included a short portion of the former freight main at North Warren. Other than a dozen miles in the Cleveland area being revitalized by the Cleveland Commercial Railroad, the balance of the Mahoning Division has either been abandoned or remains in the weeds for business that may never return.

ABOVE • A close-up view of the Huletts at the Ore Dock and River Bed Yard in April 1979 after three idle years. Note the de-trucked former M-of-W cars used as shop and storage buildings. The location would certainly make an interesting modeling project. *(Mike Kopach, ELHS Archives Collection)*

ABOVE • In February 1984 Mike captured this sobering photo showing the Huletts and other equipment being razed. The dock was never used by Conrail, which instead favored the nearby former Penn Central Whiskey Island Docks. *(Mike Kopach, ELHS Archives Collection)*

ABOVE • Another view of what was left of the River Bed Docks in February 1984. The docks were closed with the coming of Conrail in 1976 and placed for sale. The Huletts and other equipment were scrapped and the area turned into an aggregate storage yard.

(Mike Kopach, ELHS Archives Collection)

ABOVE • This April 1980 photo depicts the former HD Yard at Literary Street. Only the westbound main track remains intact. Several of the yard tracks remain in various states of disrepair and would soon be removed by a Conrail Retirement Gang with materials being reused at other locations or sold for salvage.

(Mike Kopach, ELHS Archives Collection)

LEFT • This is not post-EL yet and it's also not quite on the Mahoning Division, but we'll explain why we're showing it: Former Meadville Yard Alco S2 #518 is at Ashtabula, OH on April 12, 1975. EL sold the unit to George Silcott, a used locomotive dealer who resold it to Cleveland Electric Illuminating Co. for use at their Eastlake, OH generating station. It was later painted red, white and blue for the Bicentennial and, after being retired by CEI, it was purchased by shortline Ashtabula, Carson & Jefferson of Jefferson, OH. This photo's been included because the unit has been donated to the French Creek Valley Railroad Historical Association and is being refurbished and restored to original Erie livery and will be displayed in Meadville, near the former diesel shop along with the EL caboose.

(David H. Hamley, ELHS Archives Collection)

ABOVE • Again, this is not on the Mahoning Division post-EL but former EL GP35 #2579 now wears its Conrail number 3685 in this February 1984 photo at Collinwood. Many locomotives wore their former colors for many years before receiving the Conrail blue dip paint job. Equipment for cab signal operation on former PRR territory has been added, as evidenced by the box on the walkway in front of the engineer. *(David Kopach, ELHS Archives Collection)*

ABOVE • The former Passenger Station at Greenville stands lonely and unused in this 1999 Conrail era photo. The station was a busy location in passenger days as it served Thiel College in Greenville as well as businessmen visiting the many industries in town, which included the B&LE RR main shops and offices, Greenville Steel Car Company and Chicago Bridge & Iron Company.

Additionally, the location served as a point of travel for the Amish sect traveling to the Union City, PA or Randolph, NY area. After passenger service ended the building was used for M-of-W and C&S headquarters until closed by Conrail. NS has again reopened the building for maintenance forces. *ELHS Archives Collection)*

ABOVE • The location is Hornell Diesel Shop in March 1982. Former EL C242 #2411 sits stripped and showing its Conrail number 2485.

Conrail sold the unit in March 1978 to General Electric, which then owned the Hornell Shops where the unit was rebuilt.

(ELHS Archives Collection)

ABOVE • After the formation of Conrail, the company built a new yard on the former PRR's Salamanca Branch right-of-way paralleling the former EL at Olean, NY. The new yard was to replace Jamestown, Bradford and Salamanca yards and provide a funnel point for traffic to move four directions via the former EL and PRR. The yard was conveyed to the Western New York and Pennsylvania RR, LLC in a series of complex transactions including lease and purchase agreements to operate the former EL line from Hornell to Meadville and Oil City as well as a portion of the former PRR Buffalo Line. A collection of WNYP Alco and Montreal motive power is seen at Olean on October 12, 2007 along with a pair of leased Norfolk Southern EMD products. *(Stephen M. Timko)*

ABOVE • Twenty-five years after being conveyed to Conrail, two former Erie-Lackawanna RR Alco C424s again grace ex-EL rails. WNYP #424 (originally EL #2401) and #423 (originally EL #2407) are seen at the Falconer, NY headquarters. The new shop-office complex was still under construction in this September 2, 2001 photo. The author served as the new company's first General Manager, later being appointed Vice President & General Manager. *(Richard Borkowski, Stephen M Timko Collection)*

ABOVE • In this post-EL era photo at Brier Hill Shop, GP35 #2558 is in the company of a former PC GP9 on May 26, 1977. The gray box on the walkway in front of the engineer's window contains the cab signal equipment for former PRR lines east of Pittsburgh and on the River Line between Yellow Creek and Mingo Jct. The gray building to the right contains the crew caller, the Road Foreman, Trainmaster and the Car Foreman offices.

(David H. Hamley, ELHS Archives Collection)

ABOVE • The backdrop in this September 14, 2008 photo was the former location of the Erie Lackawanna's Brier Hill Yard. Conrail, during the downsizing of routes other than the "Big X," was eager to sell many lines to reduce labor and operating costs. In 1996, the author, while serving as Conrail Trainmaster in Youngstown, was involved in the transaction that resulted in the Brier Hill Cluster being sold to the Ohio Central Railroad. A former Conrail GP10 #7573 was brought to this location by the new owner. A former Conrail MT-4 slug is behind the locomotive. *(Stephen M. Timko)*

ABOVE • In the summer of 1996 the Ohio Central System purchased what was known as the Brier Hill Cluster from Conrail. That purchase included the former EL lines between Youngstown and Niles, plus the former EL second-subdivision between North Warren and west of Cortland. Other local former PC lines were also involved in the sale and trackage rights were given for OCS to link the lines together. Ohio Central Alco RS3 #1077 is operating on a connecting track from Girard Siding to the YS&T lead on August 31, 1998.

North Star Steel now operates a major portion of the former YS&T Brier Hill Works. The cars stored in the photo are on a short segment of former B&O trackage that allowed that line to access the Brier Hill Works from the Lake Branch. The photo location is between VO Crossover and Furnace Lane at Girard, OH. The badly mangled signal in the photo is signal 63-2M, formerly governing eastbound moves at VO Crossover. The former EL westbound main has been removed. *(David Baer)*

ABOVE • As time progressed, the Ohio Central also acquired some former Baltimore & Ohio trackage in Youngstown and became quite successful shuttling pipe from North Star Steel to the CSX interchange at nearby Ohio Junction. Dave captured Ohio Central GP10 #7591 and MT4 #1000 switching a train of empty bulkhead flat cars on August 28, 1998. At this point the former B&O Lake Branch crossed the former EL Canal Branch near Girard and the remains of the target can be seen. It was this piece of trackage that the EL used to access the Joint Yard serving U. S. Steel's Ohio Works. Interstate 80 crosses overhead and the train stretches through the manmade tunnels that carried the Pennsylvania Railroad and the Lake Erie & Eastern Railroad overhead. *(David Baer)*

ABOVE • Ohio Central SD18 #6642 shoves a cut of pipe from the former eastbound main track onto Girard Siding and then onto the former B&O Lake Branch on March 26, 2010. This move allows access to the CSX interchange at Ohio Junction about a mile to the east. The pipe was produced at V&M Star Steel Company, previously known as North Star Steel at Brier Hill. *(David Baer)*

ABOVE • Ohio Central RS3 #1077, owner Jacobson's pride and joy, pulls a train westbound (southbound on NS) under the former cantilever signal at MK Siding just east of North Warren on September 1, 1998. The Ohio Central, through aggressive marketing, was able to recapture some previously lost steel business at North Warren and for a period, retained a locomotive at Dietrich Industries, ferrying a crew to the location to perform plant switching as required. In EL days, this was the route of such hotshot freight trains as #74, 77, 98, 99 and 100's. *(David Baer)*

LEFT • The Buffalo & Southwestern Branch between BC Jct. and Waterboro was deemed excess by Conrail and was sold to the Chautauqua, Erie and Cattaraugus County's Industrial Development Agencies in order to provide rail service to local industries. The New York & Lake Erie RR is the operator of the former B&SW Branch between Gowanda and Conewango Valley, NY. A trio of Alco and Montreal locomotives handles an excursion train at South Dayton, NY on October 27, 2007. The line presently sees limited freight service. *(Stephen M. Timko)*

LEFT • In Chapter 10 we noted the challenges of operating westbound on the B&SW Branch. In this October 27, 2007 photo we see (American) Viscose #6, an 0-4-0T running westbound lite at MP 36. At this location, the "lokie" is ascending a 2.5% portion of the branch and is about to pass through the Dayton Arch where the Dunkirk Branch previously crossed overhead. A few minutes earlier, the maximum grade of 2.72% was conquered at MP 34.5. *(Stephen M. Timko)*

ABOVE • It's May 1978 and the luster has worn from SDP45 #3638, which was one of two units painted for the Bicentennial (the other being SD45 #3632). The two '45s were usually operated as a pair on EL's hot piggyback trains #99 and #100 along with similarly painted caboose C354. In this view, we see the former celebrity at the P&LE Engine Terminal at East Youngstown, OH in the company of an assortment of P&LE and former PC and EL motive power. Under a NYC-P&LE joint facilities agreement, the P&LE performed fueling and inspections as well as light maintenance on locomotives working out of the P&LE for points on NYC/PC/CR. A former EL Alco RS unit is further east near the YS&T Campbell Works footbridge.

(Ron Rohrbaugh, ELHS Archives Collection)

ABOVE • A December 1978 view at the West End of Brier Hill shows EL #2401 still in EL garb MU'ed to a trio of former PC power as they double to a caboose. The stately building to the far left is the Youngstown Sheet & Tube Company's Brier Hill Works General Office. The gray building to the right is the YS&T Yard and Scale office. The nose of an EL Alco RS unit is behind the fence along with YS&T Baldwin model S8 switcher #701.

The tall, frame-like structure near the YS&T loco is the Skull Cracking Building. It's here that the solidified iron skulls removed from ladles, old ingot molds, etc. were broken up into smaller pieces for recharging into the open hearths. The overhead crane had a magnet for moving material around and picked up a huge iron ball that was dropped to break the scrap.

(Mike Kopach, ELHS Archives Collection)

It's November 1976 and the Alco C424s have received new Conrail numbers as they tow a former PC switcher from Girard Siding through the crossovers and into the yard at the West End of Brier Hill. The Alco RS3 retains its EL number for the time being and is being shoved in this move as it will not MU to the road power.

(Mike Kopach, ELHS Archives Collection)

ABOVE • It's December 1976 and Black Monday, September 19, 1977 was in the distant future and the mills were still quite active. Former EL E8a #825 has been renumbered to Conrail #4014 and some former Penn Central switchers and GP9s have infiltrated EL territory in this photo. The Conrail general renumbering of locomotives has not made much headway yet with the other former EL power in the photo retaining their EL numbers.

(Mike Kopach, ELHS Archives Collection)

RIGHT • The tail end of Tavern Lounge Car #790 signifies the end of the train #2 at Hornell in October 1972.

(ELHS Archives Collection)

Since we've reached the east end of the Mahoning Division we're calling out the flag and bringing this volume to an end.

Thank you for riding with us on the
Erie Lackawanna's Mahoning Division.